HOMESWEET HOMEGROWN

HOMESWEET HOMEGROWN

How to grow, make and store your own food, no matter where you live.

By Robyn Jasko
Illustrated by Jennifer Biggs

HOMESWEET HOMEGROWN

How to grow, make, and store your own food, no matter where you live.

By Robyn Jasko
Illustrated by Jennifer Biggs

Edited by Adam Gnade
Designed by Joe Biel

Microcosm Publishing
2752 N Williams Ave
Portland, OR 97227
www.microcosmpublishing.com

ISBN 978-1-934620-10-6
This is Microcosm #76130

First Published May 1, 2012
First printing of 7,000 copies
Second printing of 5,000 copies January 1, 2014

Distributed by Independent Publisher's Group (IPG)

TABLE OF CONTENTS

Chapter 1: Know

WHY GROW YOUR OWN?

There are so many reasons to grow your own food these days. Whether you have a container garden in New York City or a raised bed in suburbia, you can grow your own food no matter where you live, without a huge amount of work. Because, here's a secret: gardening doesn't have to be complicated.

You take some soil and some seeds, and you make food. Making food means you don't have to go to the supermarket. By not going to the supermarket, you aren't contributing to the cycle of food transportation, fuel costs, pollution, and the absurd reality that those tomatoes you see in the store actually came from a country thousands of miles away. But that's just one reason to grow food, here's more:

Homegrown Food Tastes Better

Quite simply, food that you grow tastes a lot better because it wasn't sprayed with pesticides and it didn't sit in a truck that was driven across the country. And, by growing your own, you'll have access to culinary varieties that your regular supermarket doesn't even carry. Purple basil, heirloom garlic, yellow beets, blue pumpkins—just think of the amazing dinners!

It's Fun

Growing, making, and storing food is also rewarding, and a perfect way to add some balance to our stressed out crazy world. There are actually studies that support this—even just five minutes of putting your hands in the soil can give you a better perspective and improve your mood.

Rising Food Costs

We almost can't afford to *not* grow our own food these days. And, food costs are expected to keep going up, doubling by 2030, according to a recent study by Oxfam. Growing a small raised bed or even a few tomato plants on a balcony can save a lot of money.

You'll Know Where Your Food Comes From

No more mystery spinach—when you go out back to harvest lettuce or pick basil, you'll know for sure that it wasn't sprayed with heavy duty pesticides, or tainted with ecoli runoff from factory farms.

Kids Love Gardening

And, why not? Gardening is like magic when you think about it. But, more importantly, growing food teaches kids to be self sufficient, and to know where their food comes from. It's easy for kids to think food comes from a supermarket. That's why I love seeing children at the community garden pull up beets with a huge smile on their faces, or look in amazement at the giant pumpkin growing.

Food is power, so it's time to take matters into our own hands and start something. And this book will show you how to grow, store, and make as much food as possible on the cheap.

GROW FOR BROKE

Produce is expensive—and the costs keep going up. Especially for good organic food. Even herbs and salad greens, which can be grown on a windowsill anywhere, anytime, are $5 for a tiny box. By growing your own, you can save a lot of money, especially if you grow from seed.

Here's an example:

Cost of tomato plant:	$3 or about 25 cents if you grow it from seed
Average pounds per plant:	10 to 15
Cost per pound for organic tomatoes at the store:	$4
Cost per pound for homegrown tomatoes:	20 to 30 cents (from plants), or just 2 to 3 cents (from seed)

or, take beets:

Cost for beet seed packet:	$3 for 75 seeds
Average pounds of beets per packet:	50
Cost per pound for organic beets at the store:	$3
Cost per pound for homegrown beets:	6 cents

And, this doesn't include the high cost of heirlooms—which are usually $1 a pound more because they taste awesome and come in all sorts of different colors, shapes and sizes.

Not sure how much to grow? Check out our guide on page 17 to figure out how much to grow per person to have enough produce for the year.

HYBRID, HEIRLOOM, ORGANIC, GMO: WHAT'S THE DIFFERENCE?

There are so many terms for seeds being thrown around these days that it can be confusing to know what's what. Here's a quick lowdown:

Heirloom Seeds:

This is a true seed that has been around for at least 60 years, most likely a lot longer. Heirloom seeds are usually open pollinated, meaning that wind or insects fertilize the seed. They'll breed true to their parent plants, so if you harvest seeds and replant them you will get the same variety. Heirlooms are key to having a truly sustainable garden, since you won't have to buy seeds every year and can actually save a ton of money this way.

Hybrid Seeds:

Not to be confused with GMO (genetically modified organisms), hybrid seeds are naturally bred for beneficial characteristics such as disease and insect resistance, new flower types, improved vitamin content in vegetables and grains, and many other characteristics. The downside with hybrids is that their seed doesn't resemble the parent plant, so you cannot reliably save their seeds.

Genetically Modified Seeds (GMO)

GMOs are manmade seeds where scientists insert genetic material into a plant to add a characteristic that is not naturally there. No, it's not a Phillip K. Dick novel, this is happening now, and GMO corn, beets, and soybeans are already at your supermarket.

These seeds are highly controversial. In some parts of the world, they are outlawed. No one knows the longterm ramifications of turning nature into Frankenfood. And while the "official" word from the U.S. government is that such seeds are safe, contradictory evidence indicates otherwise.

GMO crops were created in the 1970s specifically to be resistant to Roundup—a dangerous pesticide that is produced by Monsanto, a company patenting GMO crops. See the connection? New studies are showing that the past 30 years of using Roundup on GMO crops have brought on a new breed of super weeds, which farmers are treating with even more pesticides.

More and more articles are coming out showing the irreversible health and environmental effects GMO crops are having on people and animals as they enter the food supply, but until they are outlawed, we are the guinea pigs. And that's one more reason to grow your own food.

Organic Seeds

Organic seeds are grown, saved, and stored without the use of synthetic fertilizers, pesticides, antibiotics, food additives, GMOs, irradiation, and biosolids in your food. When shopping for seeds, or for produce, choosing organic is definitely the safest way to go and a good way to keep GMOs and pesticides off your plate and out of your garden.

The Great Food Fight

There's a battle going on today for food. Between rising food costs, factory farming causing deadly ecoli runoff on vegetables, and GMOs entering the food supply, growing your own has never been more important.

Every time you buy or eat food you have a choice. And, that choice adds up. So, grow what you can, support local farmers and CSAs (Community Supported Agriculture), and help fight the good food fight!

Chapter 2: Start

STARTING FROM SEED

Some people are put off by growing from seed because they think it's too complicated, but it's not that hard at all. You'll save a ton of money versus buying plants, and have access to more varieties than you ever knew existed. Purple carrots, anyone?

Two ways to start a plant from seed:

Direct seed: When you plant the seed directly into the spot in your garden where it will grow. Easy, peasy.

Starting seeds indoors to transplant later: Some plants are frost sensitive and need to be started indoors before going into the garden. This also gives them a headstart when the plant needs a longer growing season (like tomatoes).

Starting seeds indoors is a little more involved—they'll need soil, water, and light—but it can easily be done with a greenhouse kit from the local hardware store. And, they'll look so cute growing on your windowsill!

DIRECT SEED VS. SEEDLING

It all depends on the variety. Some plants don't mind being transplanted, but the ones that do, hate it. So, it's good to know who likes what.

Vegetables to direct seed: Beans, beets, carrots, corn, garlic, kale, lettuce, melons, peas, potatoes, radishes, summer squash, spinach, winter squash, and pumpkins.
Vegetables that transplant well: Broccoli, cabbage, cauliflower, celery, eggplant, onions, peppers (sweet and chili), and tomatoes.

Seedlings aren't always faster

Take the pumpkin—if you were to plant a 3-week-old pumpkin seedling and a new set of seeds on the very same day, you'll find that the seeds will catch up and outgrow the seedling, because pumpkins get stressed out about being transplanted (and, I don't blame them). But other plants, like tomatoes, don't mind it at all.

SAVING MONEY WITH SEEDS

Growing plants from seed is definitely the cheapest way to go. Plus, you'll have access to endless varieties, instead of being at the whim of whatever your nearby plant store is selling for $3 a pop.

Here's a handy example: 1 pack of cucumber seeds (25 seeds): $2.50
1 cucumber plant: $3

Cucumbers are very quick to germinate, and super easy to plant from seed. So, if you plant your whole pack of cucumber seeds, and 20 of them make it, that's $60 worth of cucumber plants for less than the price of one plant. Plus, cucumber seeds will last for up to five years, so save any unused seeds for next year's garden.

Some seed companies like Renee's Garden and Fedco Seeds now offer variety packets so you can mix it up without spending a ton of money.

HOW LONG DO SEEDS LAST?

Seeds are living things, and if stored properly, they stay viable for five years or more depending on the variety.

Seed Shelf Life	
Type of Seed	Years
Asparagus	3
Beans	3
Beets	4
Broccoli	3
Brussel Sprouts	4
Cabbage	4
Carrot	3
Cauliflower	4
Celery	3
Chard	4
Corn	1
Cucumber	5
Eggplant	4
Kale	4
Lettuce	5
Melon	5
Onion	1
Pea	3
Pepper	2
Radish	4
Spinach	
Summer Squash	4
Tomatoes	4
Winter Squash and Pumpkins	4

Source: Iowa State University, Extension and Outreach, Department of Horticulture

STORING SEEDS:

Keep your extra seed packets in an airtight Mason jar, along with one of those little silica packets that comes in shoeboxes, and store them out of direct light. They'll stay cool and dry until you are ready to use them.

HOW MUCH TO GROW

It's easy to overplant your garden, especially if it's your first. Here's a good guideline of how much to grow per person to have enough to eat fresh, with some leftover for freezing/preserving.

Double these amounts if you want to grow enough food to last you all year long. And, definitely tweak according to what you like best:

Vegetable	Plants Per Person
Asparagus	10 to 15 plants
Beets	25 plants
Broccoli	4 plants
Beans (bush)	15 plants
Beans (pole)	3 poles
Cabbage	2 to 3 plants
Carrots	10 foot row
Cauliflower	3 to 5 plants
Celery	3 to 5 plants
Corn	15 foot row
Cucumbers	3 to 6 plants
Eggplant	3 to 5 plants
Garlic	15 to 20 cloves
Kale	3 to 5 plants
Leaf Lettuce	10 foot row
Melon	3 to 5 plants
Onions	15 to 25 plants
Peppers (hot and sweet)	3 to 5 plants
Potatoes	10 to 15 plants
Radishes	5 foot row
Spinach	5 to 10 foot row
Summer Squash	3 plants
Tomatoes	4 plants
Winter Squash and Pumpkins	3 to 5 plants

WHEN TO START YOUR SEEDS

Starting seeds is all about timing. If you start transplants too early they may be rootbound before they get outside. Too late, and they won't be ready to harvest in time. First, figure out when your first/last frost dates are, then use the guide below:

Vegetable	Weeks Before Frost to start Your Transplant Seeds Indoors	When to Plant Transplants in the Garden	Earliest you can Direct Seed before or after Last frost
Asparagus	12 to 14 weeks (from seed)	4 weeks before (for crowns)	Not recommended
Beans	Transplanting not recommended		on Last frost
Beets	Transplanting not recommended		3 to 6 weeks before
Broccoli	8 to 12 weeks	2 weeks before frost	4 weeks before
Cabbage	8 to 12 weeks	4 weeks before frost	4 to 6 weeks before
Carrots	Transplanting not recommended		4 weeks before
Cauliflower	10 weeks	4 weeks before frost	6 weeks before
Celery	8 to 10 weeks	4 weeks before frost	on Last frost
Corn	Transplanting not recommended		on Last frost
Cucumber	3 weeks	1 to 2 weeks after frost	on Last frost
Eggplant	8 to 10 weeks	2 to 3 weeks after frost	on Last frost
Kale	8 weeks before	4 weeks before frost	4 to 6 weeks before
Lettuce	6 to 8 weeks	4 weeks before frost	4 to 6 weeks before
Melons	2 weeks	2 weeks after frost	2 to 4 weeks after
Onions (seeds)	10 weeks before	4 weeks before	4 weeks before
Peas	Transplanting not recommended		6 weeks before
Peppers	8 weeks	2 weeks after frost	on Last frost
Potatoes	Does not transplant		2 to 4 weeks before
Radishes	Transplanting not recommended		4 to 6 weeks before
Spinach	Transplanting not recommended		4 to 6 weeks before
Summer Squash	3 to 4 weeks	Last frost	on Last frost
Tomatoes	6 to 8 weeks	1 to 2 weeks after frost	2 weeks before
Winter Squash	3 to 4 weeks	2 weeks after frost	on Last frost

Source: The Old Farmer's Almanac

GROW YOUR OWN SEEDLINGS

Some vegetables, like tomatoes and eggplant, need to be started earlier because they require a longer growing season.

Depending on how much time and dough you have, you can start these yourself or buy them from a local nursery.

Pros of starting your own seedings:
- [ ] Access to more seed varieties
- [ ] You'll be saving money versus buying seedlings
- [ ] Knowing your plants are 100% organic
- [ ] Satisfaction in being totally self-reliant

Cons:
- [ ] Time (caring for eggplant and tomato seedlings can be like a part-time job)
- [ ] You'll have to dedicate part of your home/apartment to lights and seed setups
- [ ] Buying soil and seed starting equipment

But, don't let this deter you—lights and seed starting equipment are a one time price to pay. It's fun to start your own plants from seed and have a little green in March.

Too busy to start seedlings?
These divas are just easier to buy:
- [ ] Tomatoes
- [ ] Eggplant
- [ ] Cauliflower
- [ ] Brussel Sprouts
- [ ] Cabbage

INDOOR SEED STARTING ON THE CHEAP

No matter where you live, you can set up a basic seed starting area without having to spend a lot of money.

Start by checking out your recycling bin—plastic yogurt containers, old salad containers and even egg shells make great seed starters.

Just make sure to poke holes in the bottom of your containers so your seeds have good drainage.

Your seeds don't need light to sprout, but they will need constant moisture and heat. Put them near a radiator or warmer spot in your house.

poke a hole for drainage!

SHINE SOME LIGHT

Once your seeds have sprouted, they will need light right away, preferably 12 to 16 hours a day. You can do this in a number of ways:

-Put them in a super sunny window and near a lamp with a CFL light at night.

-Hover a 4-foot fluorescent shop light above them. (See page 79 for an easy setup you can make at home.)

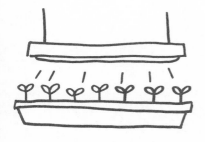

-Buy a fancy schmancy growlight kit.

If they don't get enough light, they will get leggy and tall, and will be too weak for transplanting. So hook them up!

A 4-foot hanging shop light with fluorescent bulbs costs about $35 at the local hardware store and will give your plants the light they need until they are ready to go into the garden. Plus, you can use it year after year. Florescent bulbs work well because they emit a lot of light and hardly any heat, so you won't risk burning your plants.

Also, think about where you put them. The first time I used these growlights in my upstairs window, cops were driving by my house multiple times a day, curious as to what I was growing, no doubt.

S E E D GERMINATION TIMES

Seeds germinate at different times and soil temperatures. Here's the average amount of time it takes a seed to sprout:

Vegetable	Days to Germinate	Optimum Soil Temp for Germination
Asparagus	10 to 14	75 Degrees
Beans	7 to 14	70 to 85 Degrees
Beets	7 to 10	75 Degrees
Broccoli	3 to 10	65 to 75 Degrees
Cabbage	5 to 10	68 to 75 Degrees
Carrots	12 to 15	75 Degrees
Celery	10 to 14	70 to 75 Degrees
Corn	7 to 10	75 to 85 Degrees
Cucumber	7 to 10	70 to 85 Degrees
Eggplant	10 to 12	75 to 85 Degrees
Kale/Collards	5 to 10	70 to 75 Degrees
Lettuce	7 to 10	65 to 75 Degrees
Melons	5 to 10	80 to 85 Degrees
Onions	10 to 14	60 to 75 Degrees
Peas	7 to 14	65 to 70 Degrees
Peppers, Hot	10 to 14	78 to 85 Degrees
Peppers, Sweet	10 to 14	78 to 85 Degrees
Radishes	5 to 7	65 to 70 Degrees
Spinach	7 to 14	70 Degrees
Summer Squash	7 to 14	75 to 85 Degrees
Swiss Chard	7 to 14	70 to 75 Degrees
Tomatoes	7 to 14	75 to 80 Degrees
Winter Squash and Pumpkins	7 to 14	75 to 85 Degrees

Source: Arizona Cooperative Extension, College of Agriculture, The University of Arizona.

The size of a seed helps determine how quickly it will germinate. The larger the seed, the faster it will sprout!

TIME TO TRANSPLANT

Knowing when to transplant your little seedlings outside or to larger containers is an art all in itself. Each vegetable has different growing rates and needs, but there are a few guidelines:

Look for true leaves
OK, these aren't the first set of leaves, but rather the second set, that look like what the plant will become.

Don't wait for roots to come out the bottom
This means they have been growing in the same container too long, and the roots have become tangled and are growing in circles (a.k.a. rootbound). If this happens, you'll need to break up the root before transplanting to help get those roots growing down again.

Don't wait too long to transplant
The smaller a plant is, the less shock it will experience.

Usually three to six weeks is enough time for most vegetables to be transplanted.

POTTING UP SEEDLINGS
Seedlings like tomatoes, eggplants, and peppers grow fairly quickly, so they will have to move to bigger pots before being put into the garden. Upgrade them to pots that are twice the size that they are in now so they have room to grow.

To transplant into their new pots with as little shock as possible, it'll take a little planning:

Day before:
Water your plants well the night before.

Day of:
Get your new larger pots ready. Thoroughly wet the potting soil after putting it in your new container. Only fill it halfway so the new plant has some room.

How to transplant:
Carefully lift up the plants by the first leaves and support the bottom root side with your other hand. Then, gently put them in their new container or tray.

Cover with more soil and pack it down lightly. Water thoroughly and move to a room with no lights or direct sun.

Day after:
Keep plants in the shade for one full day. This will help them put energy into their roots, not into their leaves.

MOVIN' ON UP: INTO THE GARDEN

Like people, plants need a chance to adjust to things. You can't just throw them into the garden after being in your cozy warm home for the past month—it's a mad world out there!

For one week leading up to transplant day, let them adjust gradually by bringing them outside for just a few hours, increasing the time each day.

Then, on transplant day:

☐ If possible, pick an overcast day and plant later in the day, after it cools off. This will help reduce the shock to the plant.

☐ Add some compost to the bed where they will be planted to give them a good boost.

☐ Dig a hole that is 2 inches wider and deeper than the plant's container.

☐ Place plant into the ground, disturbing the roots as little as possible.

☐ Cover the root of the plant with soil, and leave a small recessed indent at the base so the plant collects more water.

Chapter 3: Grow

Asparagus

Plant asparagus in a sunny spot once and you'll be harvesting it for the next 15 years! If done right, it will come up every spring, and be one of your first harvests.

Stats: Sunny, cold season, 2 to 3 years+, perennial, spring.

Getting Started: Buy one-year established crowns online, or at a nursery. You can save money by starting from seed, but it will take an extra year for spears to develop and can be tricky. Crowns are your best bet.

Harvest: Early spring through early June.

Companions: Dill, coriander, tomatoes, parsley, basil, comfrey, and marigolds.

Avoid Planting Near: Onion, garlic and potatoes.

Preparation: It's good to give asparagus its own bed, since it will be staying in one spot. Start prepping your asparagus bed as early as possible by double-digging and enriching it with compost.

Planting: Asparagus needs to be planted deep down to become established, so start by digging a 12-inch deep trench that's 12 to 18 inches wide. In early spring, set crowns 15 to 18 inches apart in your trench, mounding soil slightly under each plant so crown is slightly above roots. Spread roots over mound, cover crown with 2 to 3 inches of soil and water thoroughly. As plants grow, continue to put soil over crowns (about 2 inches every two weeks) until trench is filled.

Harvest: Asparagus needs to be established, so you don't want to pick it all in the beginning. Don't harvest at all the first year of planting, and harvest lightly the second. Third year on, go for it. Cut spears just under soil surface when 6 to 8 inches tall and before tips separate.

Diseases: Root rot, rust, and purple spot.

Pests: Asparagus beetles, aphids, and cutworms.

After you are done harvesting asparagus, plant tomatoes on either side. They make good pals.

Beans

Beans are some of the oldest grown vegetables on the planet, and one of the most reliable. They grow in a wide range of climates, and produce crisp snap beans or shelling beans, depending on the variety.

Stats: Sunny, warm season, 60 days for bush, 70 days for pole, summer.

Getting Started: Direct seed.

Companions: All beans do well with marigolds, potatoes, catnip, and summer savory. Interplanted bush beans thrive with carrots, beets, cucumbers, and celery, and pole beans with radishes, cucumbers, and corn.

Avoid Planting Near: Tomatoes, chili peppers, sunflowers, onions, garlic, kale, cabbage, and broccoli.

Preparation: Pole beans need trellising for support. Trellises should be 6 to 8 feet tall and sturdy enough to withstand wind and rain.

Planting: Direct seed after danger of frost is past and when soil warms. Beans can rot in cold soil. Plant several crops of bush beans 2 to three weeks apart for continuous harvest. Pole beans generally bear over a longer period of time than bush beans.

Spacing: Sow bush snap beans 4 inches apart, in rows 2 feet apart, and pole snap beans 6 inches apart, in rows 3 feet apart.

Harvest: Pick beans daily to keep plants producing heavily. Or, let beans dry out on the vine before shelling.

Diseases: Blight rust and mildew are prone to set in just before harvest as the weather heats up. Apply a natural fungicide—like a baking soda or apple cider vinegar spray—to help prevent this.

Pests: Aphids, Japanese beetles, Mexican bean beetles, rabbits, and deer.

Think outside the green bean...

Heirloom bean seeds come in a huge variety of colors and sizes, usually with an interesting story to boot.

Beets

Oh, the mighty beet! These nutritional powerhouses are reliable germinators, cold-weather tolerant, and grow just about anywhere—it's no wonder the beet has been around since the rise of Rome.

Stats: Sunny to partial shade, cold season, 45 to 80 days, spring/fall.

Getting Started: Direct seed.

Preparation: Can also sow seeds indoors about six weeks before last heavy frost and then transplant into garden in early spring.

Companions: Catnip, bush beans, onions, garlic, mint, lettuce. Interplant beets and kohlrabi for better growth.

Avoid Planting Near: Pole beans.

Planting: Sow seeds every three weeks for continuous harvest. Stop in midsummer and then seed again in fall about ten weeks before last frost.

Spacing: 2 to 3 inches between plants, 12 to 18 inches between rows.

Harvest: Pull beet roots when they are 2 to 3 inches in diameter. Any larger and they may become woody.

Diseases: Mildew and leafs spots are rare, but they do happen.

Pests: Slugs, snails, cutworms, squirrels, voles, rabbits, and deer.

Each beet seed is actually a fruit pod with a cluster of seeds. When they are about three weeks old, thin the extra beet sprouts and use them as microgreens or add to salads.

Broccoli

Everyone's favorite sidedish, broccoli is rich in vitamins A, B, and C, as well as calcium, phosphorous, and iron. And, since it's so frost hardy, you can grow it in both spring and fall.

Stats: Sunny, cold season, 50 to 90 days, spring/fall.

Getting Started: Start seeds inside six to eight weeks before planting outside, or buy seedlings.

Preparation: Broccoli likes rich, well-drained soil with lots of organic matter.

Companions: Potatoes, beets, onions, celery, Geraniums, dill, rosemary, nasturtium, and borage.

Avoid Planting Near: Mustards, tomatoes, peppers, pole beans, and strawberries.

Spacing: 15 to 18 inches between plants, in rows three feet apart.

Harvest: Cut off the main head, and then continue to harvest sideshoots all season.

Diseases: Broccoli is pretty disease resistant.

Pests: Aphids, cabbage loopers, and slugs are major culprits.

Tips: Use row covers for an even earlier harvest.

Broccoli tastes best when it has had a little frost. And don't worry about it having a central nervous system, that's a myth!!

Cabbage

Hmmm. Sauerkraut anyone? This cold weather favorite stores well and is one of the most nutritious veggies around.

Stats: Sunny, 75 days, spring/fall.

Getting Started: Transplants are way easier, but cabbage can be direct seeded five weeks before last frost.

Companions: Celery, onions, potatoes, chamomile, geraniums, dill, and rosemary.

Avoid Planting Near: Mustard greens, tomatoes, peppers, strawberries, pole/runner beans, and kohlrabi.

Preparation: For spring planting, use early varieties that mature rapidly. Late varieties are best for summer/ fall planting.

Planting: After transplanting, reduce weed competition with mulch.

Spacing: Cabbage likes some room—the closer they are planted, the smaller the heads. Space them out 15 to 18 inches between plants and 30 to 36 inches between rows for nice size heads.

Harvest: Pick when cabbage feels firm and has reached the size you want (between softball and basketball is usually about right). Heads can also be left in the garden for an extra two weeks in summer or three to four weeks in fall, just don't let them bake or freeze!

Diseases: Cabbage doesn't like humid weather and may rot in the heat.

Pests: Cabbage worms, aphids, slugs, and snails.

BTW—Cabbage has more Vitamin C than an orange!

Carrots

Super easy to grow from seed, carrots come in all shapes, colors and sizes, so look for heirloom varieties to mix it up.

Stats: Sunny to partial shade, 70 to 90 days, spring/fall.

Getting started: Direct seed.

Companions: Onions, leeks, garlic, lettuce, and rosemary. Interplant with peas, radishes, and sage to improve flavor.

Avoid Planting Near: Dill and anise.

Preparation: After transplanting, mulch to conserve water and reduce weeds.

Planting: Carrots don't love hot weather, so do your first planting early in spring. Then, plant every four weeks for continuous harvest.

Spacing: 6 inches between plants, 18 to 24 inches between rows.

Harvest: Check around the roots to see if carrots are the size you want. If so, pull up carrots with a spade. It's better to pick carrots early when they are sweetest.

Diseases: Carrots are pretty disease resistant and hardy.

Pests: Carrot rust fly, deers, voles, woodchucks, and rabbits (of course!).

Bonus: If you cover your fall carrots with straw, they'll overwinter for an early spring harvest.

Cauliflower

The diva of the vegetable garden, cauliflower has special needs, but is so worth it in the end. All you need is patience (and a few closepins) and you'll have the brightest cauliflower on the block.

Stats: Sunny to partial shade, 65 to 90 days, spring/fall.

Getting Started: You can direct sow six weeks before frost, but buying seedlings is easier.

Companions: Celery.

Avoid planting near: Tomatoes and strawberries.

Planting: Cauliflower hates transplanting, so be gentle.

Spacing: The more space you give, the bigger the heads, so give cauliflower about 15 to 18 inches between plants and 30 to 36 inches between rows for nice sized heads.

Tie it up: Although cauliflower is supposed to self blanch to keep the heads white and bright, it needs a little help sometimes (and who doesn't?) When heads are about 2 inches wide, gather up the leaves over the head and tie them up with a closepin or twine.

Harvest: Cut off entire head with a sharp knife or pruner when it reaches full size or just before.

Diseases: The head of the cauliflower will rot in hot, humid weather. That's why the clothespin trick helps.

Pests: Cutworms, cabbage worms, and loopers.

Celery

Crunch, crunch, crunch—everyone loves a little celery. This negative calorie veggie is high in nutrition, too. Some even say it has a serious calming influence and helps regulate the nervous system.

Stats: Sunny, 120 to 150 days, spring.

Getting started: Celery is tricky to start from seed, transplants are your best bet.

Companions: Cabbage family, leek, onion, spinach, and tomato.

Avoid Planting Near: Corn.

Planting: Transplant outside after all danger of frost has passed.

Spacing: One foot apart, in rows 2 to 2 1/2 feet apart.

Harvest: For a longer harvest, don't cut the entire plant. Just start by picking the outer stalks.

Diseases: Slugs, aphids, leafhoppers, and celery flies.

Pests: Fursarium wilt, leaf spot, and blight.

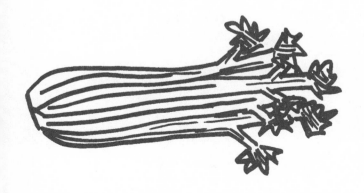

Chili Peppers

Originating in the Americas, chili peppers have been used as food and medicine since 7500 BC. They all have different levels of heat, from the totally mild, Aji Dulce, to the raging Bhut Jolokia (a.k.a. ghost pepper).

Stats: Sunny, 80 to 120 days, summer.

Getting started: Buy transplants or sow seeds indoors six to eight weeks before transplant date.

Companions: Basil and tomatoes.

Avoid Planting Near: Beans, kale, collards, and brussel sprouts.

Planting: Mulch to conserve water and reduce weed competition.

Spacing: 15 inches between plants, 30 inches between rows.

Harvest: Hot peppers will ripen and change color when they are ready to be picked. Cut peppers, don't pull them when harvesting to avoid breaking stems. If frost is coming soon, you can also pull the entire plant and hang it upside down to ripen.

Diseases: Bacterial spot, powdery mildew, and dampening off.

Pests: Slugs, snails, aphids, whitefly, and nematodes.

Corn

Popcorn, tortillas, cornbread—corn is a good old American staple. But sadly, most of the corn grown in the United States is genetically modified (86% in 2010!). Pick heirloom or organic varieties to be on the safe side.

Stats: Sunny, 65 to 100 days, summer.

Getting Started: Direct seed.

Companions: Beans, sunflowers, legumes, peas, peanuts, squash, cucumbers, pumpkins, melons, amaranth, white geranium, lamb's quarters, morning glory, parsley, and potatoes.

Avoid Planting Near: Tomatoes and celery.

Preparation: Corn gets super tall, so don't plant it where it will shade out other plants.

Planting: Corn likes friends, so plant in rows so it has support.

Spacing: 9 to 12 inches between plants and 2 to 3 feet between rows. Plant a minimum of three rows side by side to ensure good pollination.

Harvest: Sweet corn is ready for harvest about 20 days after first silks appear. Husk will be green. Not sure if it's ready? Puncture a kernel and if the liquid is clear, the corn is immature; If it's milky, it's ready to pick.

Diseases: Bacterial wilt rust and powdery mildew.

Pests: Corn ear worms, silkworms, and birds— better get that scarecrow out!

Cucumber

Originating in India, these prolific veggies come in all shapes and sizes, not just your standard green cuke. Check out heirloom cucumbers like Lemon, Poona Kheera, and Armenian cucumbers for some interesting varieties.

Stats: Sunny, 55 to 70 days, summer/fall.

Getting Started: You can buy seedlings, but direct seeding is easy.

Companions: Corn, radishes, peas, beets, carrots, nasturtiums, dill, marigolds, and sunflowers.

Avoid Planting Near: Tomatoes, potatoes, and sage.

Preparation: If transplanting, you can sow seeds indoors three to four weeks prior.

Planting: Seed after danger of frost has passed and the soil is warm.

Spacing: 12 inches between plants, 4 feet between rows; or 2 to 3 plants per hill, with hills 3 feet apart. If trellised, plant 5 seeds per foot in rows 30 inches apart.

Harvest: Can be harvested at 2 inches long to any size before they turn yellow. Harvest by turning cucumber parallel to vine and giving a quick snap.

Diseases: Cucumber mosaic, powdery mildew, and leaf spot.

Pests: Cucumber beetle and squash vine borers are the main culprits.

You can grow cucumbers vertically in smaller spaces, and have fresh cukes all summer long.

Eggplant

It's hard to believe, but until a few centuries ago, eggplant had a bad wrap, and was thought to produce insanity by Europeans. Thankfully, that's been debunked, because eggplants are downright tasty in Italian, Indian, and Mediterranean cuisines. Long live the eggplant!

Stats: Sunny, 75 to 100 days, summer.

Getting started: Transplants are easiest, or start seeds indoors eight to nine weeks before setting out.

Companions: Bean, peppers, marigolds, tarragon, and mints. Green beans especially help repel the Colorado potato beetles that love to chomp on eggplant.

Planting: Transplant after danger of frost.

Spacing: 18 to 24 inches between plants, 3 feet between rows.

Harvest: Pick early—if you leave mature eggplants on the plant they will stop producing. Look for eggplants with glossy skin that are about 2/3 their maximum size.

Diseases: Bacterial wilt and leaf spot.

Pests: Potato beetles, whiteflies, red spider mites, and aphids.

Garlic

It's no wonder Egyptians worshiped garlic and placed clay models of garlic bulbs in the tomb of Tutankhamen—homegrown garlic is worlds better than what you get in stores today. And, it's super easy to grow your own. Give it a try!

Stats: Sunny, 9 months, summer/fall.

Getting started: Score garlic cloves from a reputable nursery, or buy online. Each garlic clove becomes a new head.

Companions: Peppers, lettuce, beets, potatoes, cabbage, broccoli, kohlrabi, carrots, tomatoes, and strawberries.

Avoid Planting Near: Beans, peas, and sage.

Preparation: Garlic is planted in fall, and then harvested the next summer. (Columbus day planting and July 4th harvesting is the old adage.) So, get your beds ready at the end of September/October, and order your garlic early, because it sells out quick.

Planting: Break apart bulbs just before planting. Insert individual cloves, root side down, about 2 inches deep. Cover with dirt, and mulch with straw or leaves.

Spacing: 4 to 6 inches between cloves, 2 feet between rows.

Water: Garlic likes about 1 inch a week. It's best to withhold water two weeks prior to harvest, if possible.

Before Harvest: About four to six weeks before harvest, hardneck garlic produces a "scape" that coils. This scape is really a flower bud—you need to cut it off so the garlic puts its energy back into the bulb and they size up. Don't worry, the scapes are totally edible and delicious. Sauté them up or make pesto. Yum.

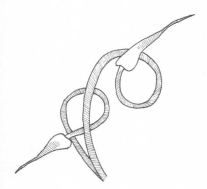

Harvest: You'll know when the garlic is ready to harvest in summer when 2/3 of the plant's leaves have yellowed. Loosen soil with a garden fork and lift, don't pull, each bulb (they may break if yanked out). Hang and cure in a dark, ventilated place for one month.

Diseases and Pests: Garlic is resistant to most diseases and pests, and can prevent Japanese beetles and deer from chomping on plants near it.

Tips: Largest cloves produce largest bulbs.

If you planted your garlic early enough in the fall, it may start shooting up early—don't worry, this is normal, and with mulch, it will overwinter and pick back up in spring.

Scapes! When you see these, cut them and make some pesto by putting them in the food processor with olive oil, parmesan, salt, and pine nuts! Scape pesto is all the rage and it even freezes well.

Kale

One of the hardiest greens around, many a peasant ancestor relied on kale to get through the winter. And, you should too— it's mighty good for you, and delicious in soups, salads, and yes, even smoothies.

Stats: Sunny, 45 days, spring, summer/fall/winter.

Getting started: Kale is easy to direct seed. Or, you can start seeds indoors and transplant into the garden four weeks before the last frost. Make repeat plantings every four weeks to have kale much of the year.

Companions: Mustard greens and catnip.

Spacing: 12 inches between plants; 24 inches between rows.

Diseases: Kale is pretty resilient to disease, which might be why it's so good for us too!

Pests: Aphids and cabbage loopers.

Harvest: To have a continuous harvest, pick the outside leaves at the base of the plant without disturbing central growing tip.

Kale can withstand temps down to 20 degrees, and even lower than that if you use a row cover. It also gets sweeter after a frost.

Lettuce

Lettuce, that quintessential vegetable, is easy to grow, great in containers, and can be harvested almost year-round. It's also one of the most pesticide-absorbant vegetables you can buy, so it's much better to grow your own organically.

Stats: Sunny to partial shade, head lettuce, 60 days; leaf lettuce, 30 days, spring/summer/fall.

Getting started: Direct seed or plant indoors, and transplant four weeks before last frost. Plant a new crop every two to four weeks for lettuce all season. Heading lettuce is easier to grow from transplants, and loose leaf types can just be direct seeded.

Companions: Radish, kohlrabi, beans, and carrots.

Avoid Planting Near: Celery, cabbage, cress, and parsley.

Spacing: Head lettuce, 12 inches between plants, 2 feet between rows; leaf lettuce, 4 inches between plants, 15 inches between rows.

Harvest: Leaf lettuce can be cut at 5 to 6 inches tall. Head lettuces can be harvested when they form a nice head.

Diseases: Too much heat and sun in the height of summer can make lettuce wilt and rot.

Pests: Slugs and bunnies.

Lettuce doesn't like the heat and may start to bolt or singe in the hottest months. Plant heat resistant varieties in June and July, or interplant long-season lettuces in summer with staked tomatoes, corn or pole beans that will shade lettuce during the hottest part of the day.

Melons

Growing melons is so much fun, and they are great to bring to summer parties. Short on space? Plant them in containers and watch them grow up your trellises or fire escape.

Stats: Sunny, 70 to 105 days, summer.

Getting started: Plant seeds directly into the garden when the soil reaches 65 degrees, or plant indoors two to four weeks before last frost. Melons germinate fast, so they will be ready to transplant when threat of frost has passed.

Spacing: Melons take up a bit of room if grown on the ground. They also like to be grown in groups. Plant melons 4 inches apart, and give 6 feet between rows so they have room to sprawl around.

Container: Plant one melon per container and give them about 4 feet or more to climb up.

Diseases: Powdery mildew and other fungus diseases.

Pests: Cucumber beetle and the squash vine borer.

Harvest: The melon will be ripe when the stem starts to dry out, and it snaps off easily when you give a twist.

it

Onions

Easy to grow and store, onions are great because they can be planted anywhere, and harvested early as spring onions.

Stats: Sunny but will tolerate some shade, 85 to 120 days, spring/summer/fall.

Getting started: Seeds should be started indoors ten to twelve weeks before last frost. If your season is not long enough for starting from seed, try sets—they are much easier to grow, and usually grow bigger onions.

Companions: Fruit trees, tomatoes, peppers, potatoes, cabbage, broccoli, kohlrabi, carrots.

Avoid Planting Near: Beans, peas, and parsley.

Preparation: Make sure soil is rich and well drained.

Spacing: Plant 1 to 6 inches apart and 1 to 2 feet between rows. You can also plant wide rows, with 4 inches between plants.

Harvest: Pick green onions anytime when the tops are 6 inches tall. For full bulbs, you'll know they are ready to harvest when 2/3 of the tops have browned and fallen over.

Eat right away, or cure for storage by leaving them out for several days to dry, then hang them in a well-ventilated room out of direct sunlight for two weeks. Leave at least 1 inch of top on when storing.

Diseases: Resistant to most diseases.

Pests: Onion fly maggot.

Tips: To grow scallions, plant onion seeds close then thin as needed.

Long Day vs Short Day Onions
On the hunt for onion seeds or sets, you'll notice most catalogues refer to long or short day onions. This is a regional thang, and you should pick onions that will grow well in your area:

Northern Gardeners: Long Day Onion
These begin to form a bulb when they get 14 to 16 hours of daylight. Varieties include Walla Walla and Red Zeppelin.

Southern Gardeners: Short Day Onions
Onion varieties like Texas Grano and Crystal Wax require will begin to bulb when there is 12 to 14 hours of daylight.

Peas
Productive and resilient, peas are one of the first vegetables you can plant in early

sprin. *Try growing snap peas up a trellis or chain link fence and then just go and munch on them right off the vine. So good!*

Stats: sunny, 50 to 70 days, spring/fall.

Companions: Carrots, cucumbers, corn, turnips, radishes, beans, and potatoes.

Plants to Avoid: Onions, garlic, leeks, and shallots.

Preparation: Treat seeds with bacterial inoculant prior to planting for better germination. Also, trellising is needed for most peas.

Planting: Direct seed in early spring.

Spacing: Plant three to six inches apart in double rows. Peas do not suffer from crowding. Double rows can be spaced two to three feet apart.

Harvest: Shelling peas and sugar snap peas are ripe when pods fill out. Pick snow peas when pods are pliable but seeds have not enlarged. Pick every day during short seasons.

Diseases: When it's hot, there is small chance of getting powdery mildew. Just use your organic fungicide spray if so (see page 75).

Pests: Birds love eating pea shoots off the vine too.

Pick peas carefully with two hands—one holding the stem and the other plucking off the pod.

Sweet Peppers

For the high price you pay for peppers at the store, you'd think they'd be hard to grow. But, they aren't tough at all, and do quite well in containers.

Stats: Sunny, 50 to 70 days, summer.

Getting started: Transplants are the easiest way, or start inside eight weeks before last frost. Peppers like it warm, so plant outside two weeks after last frost to be on the safe side.

Companions: Basil, tomatoes, geraniums, and petunias.

Plants to Avoid: Beans, kale, collards, and brussel sprouts.

Spacing: Peppers get pretty big—give them about 15 inches between plants and 30 inches between rows.

Harvest: Pick sweet peppers when they reach full size, and intended color.

Tips: Cut rather than pull to avoid breaking branches.

Diseases: Bacterial wilt or fungal problems (like leaf spots and curling). Natural fungicide to the rescue!

Pests: Cutworms and flea beetles.

Once they start fruiting, peppers get a little top heavy. Give them some love by hooking them up with bamboo supports or wire cages to keep them standing tall.

Potatoes

With origins tracing back to the Andes Mountains of South America, the potato is relatively easy to grow and doesn't take up too much space. There's even a no-dig method that just uses straw!

Stats: Sunny, 60 to 120 days, summer.

Getting started: Buy potato seeds from a reputable nursery or seed company. Choose heirloom varieties for spuds in different colors and sizes. Fingerlings are just a smaller variety of potato, and are seriously tasty.

Companion: Horseradish.

Plants to Avoid: Sunflowers, tomatoes, and cucumbers.

Preparation: If seed potatoes are the size of an egg or smaller, plant whole. Cut larger potatoes into 2-inch pieces that have 2 or 3 eyes on each piece. Cut them a day or two before you plant so they have time to cure.

Planting: Grow potatoes in soil with a pH between 5.0 and 6.0. Potatoes grown in a soil with a higher pH are prone to a disease called "scab," which produces rough spots on the potato. Adding compost or peat will help. Don't plant potatoes where tomatoes or eggplant were grown the year before. These are in the same family as potatoes and can attract similar pests and problems.

Traditional Trench Method: Dig a shallow trench, about 6 inches deep and place seed potatoes in with eyes facing up. Cover with a couple inches of soil. As they grow, gather dirt towards the center of your trench to create a hill around the leafy plant. Keep hilling for every 4 to 6 inches of new growth. Stop hilling when plants begin to flower.

Straw Bale/Mulch Method: This is one of the easiest ways to grow potatoes, and requires no digging or heavy cleaning when you harvest. First, loosen soil and lay potatoes on top. Then, cover potatoes with a good 6 inches of organic material, such as straw or leaf mulch. As plants grow, continue to hill up with mulch.

Spacing: 12 to 18 inches apart, depending on type. Fingerling plants can get quite large, so don't be deceived by their small size—all potatoes do best with 30 inches between rows.

Harvest: The entire crop is ready to harvest when the tops of the plants die back. Harvest carefully, by hand or with a shovel (definitely don't use a fork, to avoid piercing your potatoes!). Turn the soil over and search through for spuds. You can also leave the potatoes in the ground for a few weeks longer, as long as the ground is not wet.

Diseases: Blight and mildew problems happen if potato plants have poor air circulation.

Pests: Colorado potato beetles—these are not just in Colorado unfortunately!

Tip: Buy certified disease-free seed potatoes. Planting potatoes from the grocery store is a gamble. Besides the disease problem, potatoes, like many produce aisle vegetables, are often treated with a growth inhibitor to keep them from sprouting.

Harvest Cheat: New Potatoes
When the potato begins to flower, you can harvest a few small potatoes (a.k.a. new potatoes) by gently feeling around in the soil near the plant. Don't take too many—you don't want to harm the plant.

Radishes

Eaten raw, chopped in salads, or thrown in soups, radishes are pretty amazing, and ready to harvest in just a month.

Stats: Sunny/partial shade, 25 to 50 days, spring/fall.

Getting started: Direct seed all the way. Radishes are one of the easiest vegetables to grow. It's a little like magic.

Companions: Cucumbers, beans, beets, carrots, spinach, and parsnips

Plants to Avoid: Cabbage, cauliflower, brussel sprouts, broccoli, kohlrabi, turnips.

Planting: Broadcast seed, or plant in rows or blocks. With their sharp bite, radishes repel a lot of bad bugs from chowing down on your plants. Interplant radishes with cucumbers, lettuce, and carrots.

Spacing: Thin to 2 inches apart.

Harvest: Depends on variety. Round types should be harvested when they are the size of a marble. Long narrow types should be harvested when about one inch across.

Diseases: Diseases are rare for radishes.

Pests: Voles and other little critters.

Spinach

Popeye was right (of course): Spinach is a serious superfood that is packed full of nutrition and flavonoids that protect the body from free radicals. And it withstands hard frosts enough to be grown almost year-round.

Stats: Sun to partial shade, 50 to 70 days, spring/fall/winter.

Getting started: Spinach hates transplanting. Direct seed right into the garden by lightly scattering seed about two weeks before last frost. Spinach also loves the cold, so plant early spring, and late summer.

Companions: Celery, corn, eggplant, and cauliflower.

Spacing: Plant 1 inch apart in rows 2 to 3 inches apart. Plant every two weeks for continuous harvest.

Harvest: Don't cut the whole plant, instead, cut outer leaves as needed so the smaller inside leaves keep growing.

Diseases: Although diseases are rare for spinach grown in home gardens, they have been known to get powdery mildew from time to time. Avoid this by keeping leaves dry and watering at the base of plants.

Pests: Leaf miners and aphids.

Two types of spinach: **Savoy wrinkled & Smooth leaf**

Summer Squash

Now you can become that infamous neighbor who is always giving zucchini away because they have so much. Or just keep it all for yourself—it freezes well!

Stats: Sunny, 55 to 75 days, summer/ early fall.

Getting started: Start seeds indoors three weeks before frost. Transplant when danger of frost is past. Can also be direct sown six weeks after frost for a second crop.

Companions: Cucumbers, corn, beans, and radishes.

Avoid Planting Near: Potatoes.

Spacing: Plant 2 feet apart, with 4 feet between rows.

Harvest: Pick immature squash, about 6 to 8 inches long for elongated types, 3 to 4 inches in diameter for pattypans, and 4 to 7 inches for yellow crooknecks. Check plants daily once you begin harvesting, and remove old fruit so it keeps producing.

Diseases: Powdery mildew and bacterial wilt. Spray with a homemade antifungal at the first sign of problems (see recipe on page 75).

Pests: Squash bugs will love to feast on your plants, causing wilting and damage. To help avoid an infestation, check under the leaves of your squash plants just as the first flowers are developing, and every few days after for signs of eggs. If you see bright yellow or red eggs under leaves, crush them with a spoon to lower the squash bug population before it gets out of control.

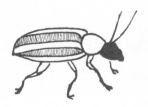

Tomatoes

Everyone's favorite, tomatoes are like the linebackers of the garden. They take up a lot of space, but these prolific plants produce fruit until frost, and are so worth it. Tomato sandwich anyone?

Stats: Sunny, 55 to 80 days, summer.

Getting started: Growing tomatoes from seed is like a part time job. They need a lot of love, lights, and watering at first, and have to to be started six weeks before last frost. Buying transplants is definitely easier, but growing from seed gives you more variety.

Planning: For tomatoes all season long, sow a second set of starts four weeks later and plant out three weeks after your first tomato planting. The second crop will pick up just as the first crop starts dying down.

Companions: Carrots, onions, basil, oregano, parsley, marigolds, garlic, celery, nasturtiums, and borage.

Avoid Planting Near: Corn, fennel, peas, dill, potatoes, beets, collards, kale, kohlrabi, cabbage, and rosemary.

Planting: Transplant when danger of frost is past. Set stocky transplants in the ground, covering stems so that only two or three sets of leaves are exposed. Stake plants as they grow up.

Spacing: Plant 30 inches apart, 4 feet between rows.

Harvest: Pick firm but fully vine-ripened fruit.

Diseases: Tomatoes are susceptible to various blights, fungal infections, and blossom end rot as the heat and humidity set in. Water at the roots to help avoid disease. They are also sensitive to tobacco mosaic virus, so wash your hands after smoking before touching the tomatoes, and don't smoke near them.

Pests: Cutworms, whitefly, earwigs, and those huge green tomato hormworms.

Tip: If transplants are leggy, plant horizontally. Roots will form along buried section of stem and produce a stronger plant.

Keep harvested tomatoes in shade. Light is not necessary for ripening immature tomatoes.

Indeterminate vs. Determinate: What's this mean?

There are two types of tomato plants:

Indeterminate tomatoes bear fruit over the entire course of a season, growing longer vines that need more support. Most heirlooms and beefstake tomatoes are indeterminate.

Determinate tomatoes have one large crop all at once. They are also more compact and don't require as much staking, making them great for smaller gardens and containers.

Winter Squash and Pumpkins

From pumpkins to spaghetti squash, winter squash have huge flowers and prolific vines that love to wrap around gardens and will even scale a roof! Check out old school heirloom varieties for some crazy looking variations and colors.

Stats: Sunny, 75 to 105 days, summer/fall.

Getting started: Winter squash can be planted indoors two to three weeks after the last frost date in your area, or direct seeded after threat of frost is past.

Companions: Corn and marigolds.

Avoid Planting Near: Potatoes.

Spacing: Winter squashes need a lot of space to sprawl around, depending on variety.

Harvest: Winter squashes are ripe when they are hard and cannot easily be pierced with a fingernail. Cut your squash about 2 inches from the vine, then set it out to cure for a few days before storing.

Diseases: Powdery mildew, bacterial wilt, and mosaic virus. Use anti-fungal sprays to prevent these from killing the plants.

Pests: Cucumber beetles, squash vine borers, and squash bugs. Spray with hot pepper/garlic sprays to keep them away.

Want to grow a ginormous pumpkin? Once a solid-looking pumpkin forms on your vine, pick the other flower buds off so the plant puts all of its energy into making one large pumpkin.

Chapter 4: Plant

GROW ANYWHERE

There are so many ways to grow food these days, you just have to pick the method that works for you and your space. You don't even have to lift a shovel if you don't want to. How much easier does it get than that?

Here are six ways to prep a garden plot so you can grow food anywhere there is sun.

Live in the city?
You'd be surprised at how much you can grow on a balcony, rooftop, or fire escape.

LASAGNA GARDENING

When *Lasagna Gardening* by Patricia Lanza came out in the late '90s, it was kind of a big deal.

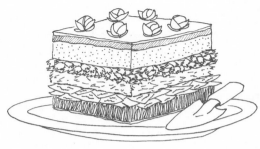

Her no-dig, no-till, no-weed method of creating a garden by layering newspaper, compost, and organic mulches on top of each other was an amazingly simple way to build a garden on top of grass or an existing bed, without lifting a shovel. And, it works.

The layers create a natural weed barrier while the organic matter enriches the soil to make one kick ass garden bed.

How to Make a Lasagna Garden

Start by choosing a sunny spot where you want to build your lasagna bed. Wet some black and white newspaper sections, and layer them right on top of the lawn in the shape of your new garden or bed, at least five pages deep.

Then, start layering your organic ingredients to build up the bed as high as you want. Water again. Then, plant directly into the lasagna bed and add mulch around your plants. Insta-garden.

Ingredients to Layer for a Lasagna Bed

- Newspapers (black and white, non glossy sections, soy-based ink only)
- Chopped leaves
- Grass clippings
- Compost
- Animal manure
- Coffee grounds
- Straw
- Wood ashes
- Sphagnum peat moss

Many of these ingredients are readily available and, even better, they're free.

DOUBLE DIG IT

Unlike lasagna gardening, double digging is a ton of work, but it pays off in the long run by giving you one of the most primo garden beds you've ever had. Similar to a raised bed, double digging takes it a step further by going 2 feet deep into the soil, giving plant roots plenty of room to stretch out.

Made popular by John Jeavons' book *How to Grow More Vegetables*, double digging creates a deeply aerated, enriched bed that kicks out more vegetables in smaller spaces.

How to Double Dig:

1. Get a friend to help.

2. Dig a trench 12 inches deep (about one shovel-length) the length of your planting area, and save that soil in a wheelbarrow.

3. Loosen the soil at the bottom of the trench and dig in another 12 inches (hence the name, double dig).

4. Add organic material, such as compost, and any necessary soil amendments. (A spading fork works well for this).

5. Dig a second trench parallel to the first trench.

6. Use the topsoil from the second trench to fill the first one, adding more organic matter and mixing it in.

7. Keep double digging the rest of your garden. Use the wheel barrow soil from step 1 to fill in the last trench.

fig.4:

Then, plant, water, and crack open a beer because that was a lot of work.

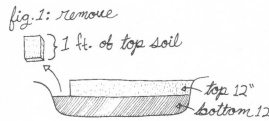

fig. 1: remove

} 1 ft. of top soil

top 12"

bottom 12"

How to Remove a Lawn

If you are starting a new bed the double dig way, you'll have to remove the grass first.

Removing the thick carpet of suburbia is no easy task, but there are better ways to do it.

fig. 2: loosen it up!

1. Water the area a few days ahead of time to loosen it up.

2. Cut the sod in parallel strips with a flat-end spade.

3. Lift up one end and roll it up.

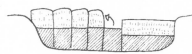

fig. 3: double - digging

4. You are ready to start digging or rototilling your plot.

What to do with the grass?

You can either compost it or just let it break down. If you start early enough (say the fall before, or as soon as the ground thaws) pull out the grass, square by square, and flip it upside down, so the dirt side is facing up. The grass will decompose in about a month, and add lots of organic matter back into the soil. Once it breaks down, dig in.

RAISED BED GARDEN

A raised bed is a method of gardening where you contain your garden within a framed structure, add dirt, and plant. You can put these right on top of the lawn, and they make gardening look nice, neat and contained (if you are into that sort of thing).

There are lots of pros to going with the raised bed route—no digging, minimal weeding, and loose soil that is great for growing everything, especially root vegetables.

Raised bed gardens are also a good option if you don't have the best soil since you add your own topsoil, compost, and amendments.

You can customize a raised bed to fit your space by building one with wood or buy a prefab raised bed kit from the interweb or a seed catalog.

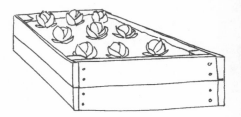

PLANT-IN-A-BAG GARDEN

This is probably the easiest no-dig, no-weed, no-brainer way to grow anything that exists. It's also a good fix for people that are super busy, super lazy, or stuck with lousy soil. And, although it looks a little hardcore, you'll be loving those homegrown tomatoes in August when everyone else is paying $8 a pound for heirlooms.

You can make and plant this soil bag in about 60 seconds.

Step one: Get a bag of organic potting soil and lie it flat wherever you want to have a bag of soil with a plant growing in it. Good places include: fire escapes, patios, and rocky areas of your yard.)

Step two: Cut a few slits for drainage on the bottom and a square out of the top.
Step three: Plant your plants. Add water.

That's it. You don't want to overcrowd these—one tomato per bag, or up to four pepper plants. Or, load it up with lettuce, herbs, swiss chard, radishes, whatever you like. The bag will retain moisture better than a container, so you won't have to water as much, just once a week.

Class up your soil bag by putting straw mulch, big rocks, or painted wood boards around it.

STRAW BALE GARDENING

A step up from the bag garden, straw bale gardening is another great no-dig method that reduces weeds, watering, and gives you perfect soil for growing anything. Plus, it's raised off the ground so critters are less likely to chow down on your lettuce.

Start by getting a few straw bales. Not, hay—hay has seeds in it that may sprout (and hay is for *horses*). Your straw bale should have twine around it. Leave this on.

Place the straw bale in a sunny spot, wherever you want your garden. Then, soak it good with a hose. This will make it super heavy, so don't plan on moving it after you water it. Leave the bale outside for 5 days or so and let it heat up in the sun so the straw starts to break down a bit. You can also add compost tea to the top to add nutrients into the straw.

After 4 days, the straw should have broken down a bit. Break up the top of your bale with a trowel and remove about six inches of straw from the inside of the top. Replace with organic soil and compost. Plant! Then water like you would a regular garden.

Finding straw bales

I buy my straw bales at the laundrymat; where they also sell buffalo meat—don't ask. I live in a quirky town. Point is, once you start looking for straw bales you will find them. Check nurseries, local farms, the paper, craigslist, garden centers, or feed supply stores. They should be three to five bucks a piece.

CONTAINER GARDENING

You don't have to be a slave to Whole Foods anymore—you can easily grow a surprising amount of your own organic food in a small space. Do it!

Containers are the perfect option for city gardeners since they take up so little room, and can be grown anywhere there is sun—fire escapes, rooftops, balconies, patios, front sidewalks, you name it.

Almost any vegetable can be grown in a container, but it's important to get varieties that are bred for smaller spaces. With the rise in urban gardening, some seed catalogs even have complete sections and seed collections dedicated to containers. Look for varieties with almost seemingly condescending names like: "dwarf", "mini", "baby", "bush", "little" for varieties bred for smaller spaces.

Think Outside the Terra Cotta

Containers come in all shapes and sizes—you can even reuse soup and bean cans, kitty litter tubs,

or whatever else you want to pilfer from your nearby recycling bin. Have fun with it.

The Topsy Torture

OK, we've all seen the infomercials—the Topsy Turvy makes it possible to grow plants upside down, in space, anywhere, just like magic! But, is this technology being used for good? Read *The Secret Life of Plants* and get back to me on that one...the Plant in a Bag is much nicer to your tomato plants and they will love you for it.

Chapter 5: Plan

MAKE A PLAN

Before you start, it's helpful to make a plan of attack. First, scope out your yard or growing space—does it get 6 to 8 hours of sun a day? Is there a fence that you can use as a trellis for cucumbers? A little planning can go a long way. Drawing out a garden plan (in pencil first) is a helpful way to get a good idea of your space, and what kind of food you plan on growing.

CHOOSING WHAT GROWS BEST IN YOUR SPACE

Each plant has different needs—while some love a little bit of shade and part sun, others require 8 hours of sun a day to grow. Here's who likes what:

Plants that love sun (6 to 8 hours)
- Asparagus
- Beans
- Celery
- Cucumbers
- Melons
- Peppers
- Onions
- Squash (winter and summer)
- Tomatoes

Shadier plants (3 to 6 hours of sun)
- Beets
- Beans
- Broccoli
- Cauliflower
- Carrots
- Kale and Leafy Greens
- Lettuce
- Peas
- Brussels Sprouts
- Radishes
- Swiss Chard

The Three Sisters

This Native American tradition of planting corn, beans, and squash together is a prime example of interplanting and companion planting put to good use.

The corn grows tall and becomes a trellis for the pole beans. The beans replace the nitrogen in the soil used by the corn, and the winter squash rambles around below to suppress weeds.

WHAT GROWS WHEN

Unlike the supermarket, where you can buy anything at anytime, each vegetable has a preferred season that it is grown and harvested in, depending on the climate.

Although this may at first seem inconvenient if you have never thought to eat seasonally, you'll notice that food grown locally and in season tastes so much better. Ever had a tomato from the supermarket that tasted like cardboard in December? Start eating seasonally and you'll get the best tasting, most nutritious food around.

Spring	Summer	Fall
• Asparagus	• Eggplant	• Brussel Sprouts
• Beets	• Melons	• Beets
• Broccoli	• Tomatoes	• Cabbage
• Cabbage	• Squash (Summer and	• Carrots
• Carrots	Winter)	• Celery
• Cauliflower	• Swiss Chard	• Cucumber
• Celery		• Kale
• Cucumbers		• Lettuce
• Kale/Swiss Chard		• Radishes
• Lettuce		
• Onions		
• Peas		
• Radishes		
• Spinach		

Planting a Second Crop

During the height of the summer, plant a fall crop of cucumbers, cauliflower, kale, cabbage, beets and broccoli—by the time they mature, the temps will have cooled down a bit and you'll have a second harvest in time for Thanksgiving.

SPACING PLANTS

OK, so you've decided what you want to plant, now the question is how many plants can fit in your garden. Those cute little tomato plants you take home can grow to be huge bullies of the garden, so you have to space appropriately so they don't end up overcrowding each other by August.

Mel Bartholomew, the author and guru of the *Square Foot Gardening* movement, has a simple method for spacing out plants based on 12 by 12-inch squares.

Plants that need 12 inches of space:

Asparagus, broccoli, cabbage, cauliflower, corn, eggplant, melons, peppers, squash, and tomatoes.

Plants that need six inches of space:

Heading lettuce, cucumbers, potatoes, swiss chard, and kale.

Plants that need 4 inches of space:

Beans (bush), beets, celery, garlic, onion, and spinach.

Plants that need 3 inches of space:

Beans (pole), carrots, leaf lettuce, peas, and radishes.

You can use the same guidelines above for containers, but choose 20 inch containers to give plants a little more room (e.g., 1 tomato plant, or 14 radishes per 20 inch container).

INTERPLANTING

If you are short on space, interplanting can help you get more out of your garden by matching up plants based on light requirements, root systems, nutrient needs, and growth speed. It also means there is less room for weeds.

Sounds like a complicated puzzle, but with a little planning, you can get a lot more out of your garden using this common sense method.

InterPlant _____	with _____
Asparagus	Parsley, tomatoes, Lettuce, or spinach
Beans	Celery, radishes, tomatoes, corn, or squash
Beets	Brussel sprouts, cabbage, kohlrabi, or onions
Broccoli	Beans, onions, or potatoes
Cabbage	Celery, onions, peppers, potatoes, or tomatoes
Carrots	Cabbage, leeks, onions, peas, or radishes
Cauliflower	Lettuce, spinach, or celery
Celery	Beans
Corn	Beans, lettuce, or potatoes
Cucumbers	Celery, Chinese vegetables, lettuce, or okra
Eggplant	Celery, onions, beans, or spinach
Garlic	Cabbage, tomatoes, or garlic
Kale	Radishes
Lettuce	Broccoli, carrots, onions, corn, parsnips, radishes, cucumbers, cauliflower, or tomatoes
Melons	Bush beans, corn, or radishes
Onions	Beans, beets, cabbage, carrots, eggplant, lettuce, peppers, radishes, or spinach
Peas	Beans, cabbage, carrots, lettuce, radishes, spinach, or turnips
Peppers	Carrots, onions, or basil
Potatoes	Onions
Radishes	Beans, lettuce, melons, onions, peas, or swiss chard

Source: National Sustainable Agriculture Information Service

Interplant _____	with _____
Spinach	Broccoli, beans, brussel sprouts, cabbage, cauliflower, eggplant, or onions
Tomatoes	Carrots, lettuce, onions, or basil
Squash, summer	Bush and pole beans, or corn
Squash, winter	Bush beans or corn

Carrots have deep root systems so they make excellent partners for cabbage or onions, which grow above ground.

COMPANION PLANTING

While interplanting is all about getting more out of your space, companion planting takes it a step further, pairing up vegetables that improve each other's growth patterns and their ability to fight off bad insects or diseases.

Like people, it means that some plants are better suited for each other. These dynamic duos work together on a physical level to become power couples of the garden.

Vegetables	Friends	Not Friends
Asparagus	Dill, coriander, tomatoes, parsley, basil, comfrey, and marigolds	onion, garlic, and potatoes
Beans	All beans: marigolds, potatoes, catnip, summer savory, Bush: carrots, beets, cucumbers, and celery, Pole: radishes, cucumbers, and corn	Tomatoes, chili peppers, sunflowers, onions, garlic, kale, cabbage, and broccoli
Beets	Catnip, bush beans, onions, garlic, mint, and lettuce. Interplant beets and kohlrabi for better growth.	Pole beans
Broccoli	Potatoes, beets, onions, celery, geraniums, dill, rosemary, nasturtium, and borage	Mustards, tomatoes, peppers, pole beans, and strawberries

Vegetables	Friends	Not Friends
Cabbage	Celery, onions, potatoes, chamomile, geraniums, dill, and rosemary	Mustard greens, tomatoes, peppers, strawberries, pole/runner beans, and kohlrabi
Carrots	Onions, leeks, garlic, lettuce, and rosemary. Interplant with peas, radishes and sage to improve flavor.	Dill and anise
Cauliflower	Celery	Tomatoes and strawberries
Celery	Cabbage family, leek, onion, spinach, and tomato	Corn
Corn	Beans, sunflowers, legumes, peas, peanuts, squash, cucumbers, pumpkins, melons, amaranth, white geranium, lamb's quarters, morning glory, parsley, and potatoes	Tomatoes and celery
Cucumbers	Corn, radishes, peas, beets, carrots, nasturtiums, dill, marigolds and sunflowers	Tomatoes, potatoes, and sage
Eggplant	Bean, peppers, marigolds, tarragon and mints. Green beans especially help repel the Colorado potato beetles that love to chomp on eggplant.	None
Garlic	Peppers, lettuce, beets, potatoes, cabbage, broccoli, kohlrabi, carrots, tomatoes, and strawberries	Beans, peas, and sage
Kale	Mustards and catnip	Bush and pole beans, and strawberry
Lettuce	Radish, kohlrabi, beans, carrots	Celery, cabbage, cress, and parsley
Melons	Corn, pumpkin, radish, and squash	Potatoes
Onions	Fruit trees, tomatoes, peppers, potatoes, cabbage, broccoli, kohlrabi, or carrots	Beans, peas, and parsley

Source: Cornell University Cooperative Extension, Chemung County and National Sustainable Agriculture Information Service

Vegetables	Friends	Not Friends
Peas	Carrots, cucumbers, corn, turnips, radishes, beans, and potatoes	Onions, garlic, leeks, and shallots
Peppers, Chili	Basil and tomatoes	Beans, kale, collards, and brussel sprouts
Peppers, sweet	Basil, tomatoes, geraniums, and petunias	Beans, kale, collards, and brussel sprouts
Potatoes	Horseradish, cabbage, corn, and peas. Eggplant can be a trap crop.	Cucumber, pumpkin, squash, sunflowers, and tomatoes
Radishes	Cucumbers, beans, beets, carrots, spinach and parsnips	Cabbage, cauliflower, brussels sprouts, broccoli, kohlrabi, and turnips
Spinach	Beans, celery, corn, eggplant, and cauliflower	Potatoes
Squash, summer	Cucumbers, corn, beans, and radishes	Potatoes
Squash, winter	Corn and marigolds	Potatoes
Tomatoes	Carrots, onions, basil, oregano, parsley, carrots, marigolds, garlic, celery, nasturtiums, and borage	Corn, fennel, peas, dill, potatoes, beets, collards, kale, kohlrabi, cabbage, and rosemary

roomies

Chapter 6: Make

CREATE YOUR OWN SEEDLING POTS WITH NEWSPAPER

After your seeds have started, these easy-to-make newspaper pots are perfect for transplanting your new seedlings. Forget pricey plastic sets—all you need is some extra newspaper and a small cup or Mason jar and you are on your way.

Get:
- A bunch of newspaper

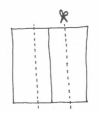

Step 1.
Cut sheets of black and white newspaper in half or thirds, depending on the size of pot you want to make. Make sure not to use pages with color, since this will be going directly into your garden. (Color newspapers may contain unsafe heavy metals).

Step 2.
Align your Mason jar or cup with the newspaper so that a few inches of paper are above the opening of the cup. Roll the newspaper so it circles the cup.

Step 3.
Push the sides of the paper that are above the cup's rim inside, so they are wrapped inside the top of the glass.

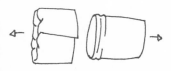

Step 4.

Remove the cup gently, while still keeping the pot's shape.

Step 5.

Use the bottom of the cup to reinforce the pot's bottom by inserting it inside the newspaper pot. Tamp down the inverted ends, so it seals the bottom.

ta da!

Step 6.

Add soil and transplant or start your seedlings.

When they reach the size for transplanting outside, they can be placed directly into your garden. This will also alleviate root disruption for healthy, happy seedlings!

EASY DIY RAIN BARREL

Save water, save time, and save money by making your own rain barrel this year.

No need to shell out hundreds of bucks for those rainbarrels in catalogues—you can make one on the cheap with a single trip to the local hardware store.

Get:
* 55 plastic gallon barrel with an opening and stable base
* Downspout extender
* 3/4" faucet
* Roll of teflon tape
* Caulk
* Garden hose

To construct your barrel:

Rain barrels work best if you have a roof to collect water off of (metal roofs work great).

Once you've decided which downspout you'd like to place your rain barrel near, cut the downspout and add the extender. This will then go directly into your barrel.

Cut a hole in the top of the barrel that is large enough for the downspout extender to fit inside.

Drill a 1" hole towards the bottom of your barrel with a hole saw or drill bit where you want your spigot, just off the bottom of the container.

Add your spigot

To attach your 3⁄4" faucet, wrap the threads in tape, caulk the taped thread and insert into the drilled hole. Once it's where you want it, caulk the area inside and outside the spigot well to reduce leakage and let set. If you want to skip this caulking step, get a spigot that just fits right into the 1" hole.

Place your new rain barrel under your downspout extender and wait for rain! When it fills up enough, just turn your spigot and water away.

SIMPLE SEED TAPE

No more fumbling with teeny tiny seeds or crowded rows of carrots! This easy seed tape will help you save seeds, eliminate thinning, and completely decompose in your garden while helping you score perfect rows. Oh, and they are fun to make and give as gifts.

Get:
*   1/4 cup organic flour and enough water to make a paste
*   Strips of paper (black and white newspaper, single-ply toilet paper, a paper towel, or a thin paper bag all work)
*   A paint brush or toothpick for dabbing drops of the paste
*   Seeds! This works great for carrots, radishes, lettuces, flower onions—anything teeny tiny. You can also mix it up and make a companion or interplanting row to be fancy (e.g., alternating carrots, lettuce, and radish seeds).

Step 1.
Cut your paper up into strips.
Step 2.
Add just enough water to the flour mixture to make a paste.
Step 3.
Dip your toothpick or paintbrush into the flour mixture and make dots on the paper where you want to put your seeds.
Step 4.
Let it dry overnight. Then, roll up, label, and store in an airtight coffee can or glass Mason jar.

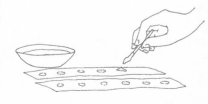

MAKE A PALLET COMPOSTER

Turn those extra kitchen scraps and leaves into rich compost that your garden will love!

Get:
- 4 wooden pallets of equal sizes
- Metal hinges
- Wooden stake or fence post
- Nails
- A latch

Step 1. Take a pallet and stand it on its long edge to form the back edge of the compost bin. Using a sledgehammer, push a wooden stake or fencepost through the two layers of the pallet at either end for stability.

Step 2. Position the remaining two pallets at right angles to the first to make the sides,

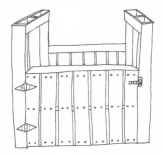

butting the corners tightly together to stop compost spilling through the gaps. Fix in place with stake or fencepost like in step 2.

Step 3. Add metal hinges at each corner to reinforce the bin. For the door, use a metal hinge on one side of the last pallet to make a gate.

Step 4. Add a latch to the other side so you can keep it shut. Add compost and turn often!

HOMEMADE BUG, WEED KILLER, AND ORGANIC PLANT SPRAYS

Forget about using deadly Roundup or chemical treatments on your plants (if it kills every type of bug and weed, imagine what it does to people). It defeats the purpose of growing vegetables if you are going to poison your food.

Everything you need to treat your plants can be found in your kitchen. These are effective, people safe, and environmentally friendly.

Natural Weed Killer

Get:
* Tea kettle
* Water

Boil water.
Pour hot water over weeds.
Done! It will kill them within hours.

Vinegar Weed Spray

* 5% of vinegar or higher
* Spray bottle

Spray the vinegar on leaf foliage on a sunny day and it'll zap those weeds.

Natural Bug Spray

Good for warding off cucumber, potato beetles, squash bugs, hornworms, rare loopers, aphids, and flea beetles.

* 5 garlic cloves
* 2 Tbsp hot pepper flakes or one habanero pepper
* 2 cups of water
* 1 onion
* 1 tsp organic liquid soap

Blend concoction and let it sit a day or overnight in a glass jar. Using gloves, strain with a coffee filter. Add 1/2 cup of concentration into a spray bottle and fill the rest of the bottle with water. Apply to any type of plants where bad bugs are attacking. Be careful to not get this one in your eyes!

Just be careful—these methods are not discerning, and they will kill your favorite plants and good bugs too.

ANTIFUNGAL SPRAYS
Apple Cider Vinegar Fungicide

Good for getting rid of leaf spot, mildew, and scab. If you have pepper plants with leaves curling inward, this will help you out.

Mix:
3 Tbsp of cider vinegar (5% acidity)
1 gallon water

Spray in the morning on infested plants.

*Baking Soda Spray

Use for anthracnose, early tomato blight, leaf blight and spots, powdery mildew, and as a general fungicide.

Mix:
1 Tbsp baking soda
2 1/2 Tbsp vegetable oil
1 gallon of water

Shake this up and then add 1/2 tsp of organic castille soap (Like Doc Bronner's) and spray at the plant's base and on all sides of leaves and stems. Repeat every 5 to 7 days as needed.

*Source: Cornell University

MAKE COMPOST TEA

Give your plants a jolt of superfoods by making this concentrated compost tea. Good for improved disease/pest-resistance, and to have a stronger garden overall.

It's like brewing a big mug of compost coffee!

Step 1. Get a 5 gallon bucket and a small bag of compost.

Step 2. Mix together.

Step 3. Add an aquarium pump to get some aeration.

Step 4. Let it bubble for 24 hours.

Step 5. Strain through a large cloth and throw solids into the garden.

Use the liquid compost tea on plants and they will love you for it!

No aquarium pump? It'll just take a little longer—stir the bucket every day to give it some anaerobic activity, and it'll be ready in a week. Spray on plants or water directly at the roots.

BUILD A STRAW BALE RAISED BED/COLD FRAME

Put your shovel down—this straw bale raised bed makes an instant, affordable, three season garden that you can put anywhere there is sun. And, it costs less than $20 to make (which translates to about 5 minutes shopping in the organic produce aisle.)

Get:
* 4 straw bales
* Organic soil (a mix of topsoil or compost is good)
* Old windows (make sure they don't have paint on them, you don't want that to chip off into your coldframe!)

Make:

Arrange four strawbales in a square. Add soil or compost inside square to cover and establish a nice raised bed. Then, when it gets cold (in the 40s), kick your straw bales into transformer mode by adding windows and making it a coldframe.

The straw insulates the coldframe so your late summer planted greens and seeds will kick it out all winter in warmer climates, or, go dormant and come back to life in early March. Either way, you'll have greens long after everyone else has put their shovels away for the season.

Then, when it warms up, remove the windows and use as a raise bed. Repeat again in fall. Save tons of dough.

MAKE A SEED STARTING STATION OUT OF AN OLD BOOKCASE OR DRESSER

Starting your own seeds can save a ton of money. But, they'll need some good light. Hack together this space-saving diy seed starting station for as little as 15 dollars.

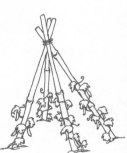

Get:
- An old bookshelf or dresser (remove the drawers of the dresser)
- A shop light fluorescent fixture that fits inside the bookshelf or dresser shelves

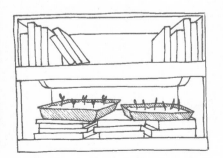

Make:
Screw the fluorescent shoplight right into the underside of the top shelf or dresser compartment.

Seedlings need to be close to the light, so add books underneath to get them about 4 inches away. Take books away as seedlings grow.

HOW TO MAKE DRIP IRRIGATION OUT OF AN OLD HOSE

This is a great way to repurpose an old hose so you can custom water your garden by just hitting a switch. Plus, directly watering a plant at the roots will save a ton of water, and prevent fungal diseases spread by soggy, damp leaves.

Get:
- And old hose, or multiple old hoses to water your garden
- A drill
- Small drill bit
- End cap
- Marker

Make:
Step 1.
Position the hose at ground level where you want your plants watered.

Step 2.
Mark an x on the base of the hose where plants are so you can drill a hole to water them.

Step 3.
Drill a hole at the x's—be sure the hole is big enough for water to flow, but not so big that you get a huge puddle. Keep holes even sizes.

Step 4.
Attach an end cap at the end of the hose.

Step 5.
Attach the other end of the hose to a water source.

Step. 6.

Mulch the top of the hose with straw to keep moisture in.

Step 7.

Give it a go. Tweak as needed. Make sure not to leave it on, you don't want to drown your plants!

Chapter 7: Eat

RECIPES INDEX
Mixed Veg: Freeform Recipes to Use Up Whatever Vegetables You Have Around

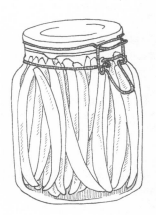

Garlic
- Roasted Garlic Spread
- Quick Garlic Bread

Kale
- Kale Chips
- Kale Tacos

Lettuce
- 3 Quick Salad Dressings

Melons
- Melon Yum Yum
- Quick Blender Melon Sorbet

Peppers
- Orange Crush Habanero Sauce

Potatoes
- Beltzville Roasted Potatoes

Summer Squash
- Steph's Johnny Cakes
- Zucchini Pasta

Tomatoes
- Easy, Amazing 20 Minute Tomato Sauce
- Puttanesca Sauce
- Jeri's Tomato Pesto

Winter Squash
- Pumpkin Gnocci
- Spaghetti Squash Bowls

EAT

Unlike supermarket produce, most likely grown in some far away country and trucked thousands of miles to get to your cart, organic produce that you grow yourself will taste better, be more nutritious, and save you money. Don't forget to eat it! Here are some flexible recipes for ways to use up whatever you have growing, and some recipes to use up a lot of vegetables that have become staples in our house.

Switching out ingredients
Make all these recipes your own (e.g., to make things vegan, swap butter for Earthbound margarine or olive oil). Hate parsley? Try cilantro. Cooking is about having fun—and since you already have the best ingredients on earth, your food is going to be totally flavorful.

MIXED VEG

These recipes are great to use up a ton of vegetables, and are flexible to whatever you have in the fridge or fresh from the garden. Plus, the chili, curry, and soup recipes store well, so make a huge vat and freeze the extra in quart size, large mouth glass Mason jars. Then, the next time you have a late day at work or don't feel like making dinner, thaw one of these suckers and you're set. It's a lifesaver to have amazing, fresh, healthy food ready to go in your freezer.

How to defrost a Mason jar quickly
Take your frozen Mason jar and put it in a large bowl of warmish water (don't make it too hot or the jar may crack). Make sure most of the jar is submerged. Soak it for about 30 minutes to an hour and then it should be defrosted enough to empty into your pan. Heat up soup/chili/curry sauce on the stovetop until hot, and you're good to go.

SOUPS
Italian Soup

Ingredients:
- Olive oil
- Stock: onions, garlic, chopped tomatoes, water
- Vegetables (use any or all): zucchini, cauliflower, greens, peppers, cabbage, asparagus, mushrooms, carrots, spinach,

etc.
- Protein: beans, lentils, or chickpeas
- Spices: fennel, basil, parsley, thyme, oregano, salt and pepper to taste

In a large soup pot, add stock ingredients, cover with water, and cook until it starts to boil. Then add rest of the ingredients, and lower to a simmer for ten minutes. Taste and adjust spices accordingly. Get crusty bread ready!

Adding pasta
Want to make a soup with pasta? Cook the pasta in a separate pot first, then add it to your soup in the last step.

Cream of _____ Soup

Potatoes make this simple creamy broth delicious and dairy-free. Customize it by adding whatever main veggie you want to fill in the blank.

Ingredients:
- 2 Tbsp olive oil
- Stock: onions, celery, garlic, 4 to 5 potatoes, water, a couple of vegetarian bouillon cubes
- Vegetables (use any one): zucchini, cauliflower, spinach, peppers, broccoli, asparagus, or mushrooms
- Spices: cilantro, parsley, or thyme, salt and pepper to taste

JeRRi BLank Loves it!

Heat up olive oil in your soup pot. Add onions, celery, and garlic for 5 minutes. Add potatoes and sauté for two more minutes. Then, add water to cover the potatoes and simmer for 15 minutes until they are soft. Add your vegetable and let simmer 5 minutes more. Remove half of the soup and blend it up. Pour back in to the pot. (Or, get out the immersion blender and just blend it partially, whatever is easier). Add spices to taste.

Optional: Add a bit of soy/nut/cow's milk/cashew cream, butter, or Earthbound margarine if you want it creamier.

Garlic Soup

Great for fighting a cold, or if you just need a comforting, warm soup. This one is a medicinal powerhouse, but tastes amazing.

Ingredients:

*   2 Tbsp olive oil
*   Stock: onions, celery, carrots, head of garlic, ginger, water
*   Vegetables (use any or all): cabbage, sweet potatoes, spinach, collards, kale, zucchini
*   Protein: red lentils
*   Spices: curry, fresh cilantro, salt and pepper to taste

Heat up olive oil in a soup pot and sauté onions, carrots, sweet potatoes (if using), and celery until softened. Add garlic and simmer for another minute. Add water to cover, add lentils and heat until it boils. Lower heat, add greens and spices and simmer until it's all softened. Add fresh cilantro if you want.

Curry

Curry is a great dish to use up whatever is in the fridge, and makes a great cold-weather meal that tastes even better the next day. Just add some Indian pickle and naan bread or rice and you are set. Look for curry paste at your local Indian grocery, or in the ethnic food aisle of your grocery store. Patak's is the best off the shelf brand if you are in a rush.

Ingredients:

*   Base: onions, 6 chopped tomatoes, (or 28 oz. can), equal amounts of minced garlic and ginger, olive oil or ghee if you have it
*   Vegetables (any or all): sweet potatoes, winter squash, cauliflower, peppers, carrots, broccoli, spinach, potatoes, green beans, zucchini, etc.
*   Curry spices: 2 Tbsp each of cumin and coriander powder, 1 Tbsp cumin seeds, 1 tsp turmeric, pepper flakes to taste
    (Or, a few tablespoons of Patak's curry paste)
*   Fresh cilantro to garnish

Heat up oil in a pot, and cook onions until softened. Add garlic, ginger, and cumin seeds for another minute. Then, add rest of spices (or curry paste) and let cook for a few more minutes. Add tomatoes, vegetables, and water to cover and let it simmer until everything is softened, about 20 minutes. Add more spices if needed, and throw in chopped cilantro. Garnish with yogurt, naan, rice, Indian pickle and/or chutney. Yum.

Ramp up the protein by adding garbanzo beans.

Chili

A great way to use a bunch of vegetables—and it freezes well.

Ingredients:
* Olive oil
* Base: onions, 6 chopped tomatoes (or 28 oz. can), garlic
* Vegetables (any or all): peppers, mushrooms, zucchini, carrots, kale, broccoli, spinach, green beans
* Beans
* Chili Spices: chili powder, cumin, hot pepper flakes to taste
* Flavors: espresso/finely ground coffee, dark chocolate, chipotle peppers

Heat up oil in a large pot. Add onions until soft, then garlic for another minute. Then, add tomatoes, vegetables, beans, and spices you'd like. Add water to cover and let simmer until all is soft, about 20 minutes.

Vegetable Stirfry

These simple stirfry recipes can be made in 30 minutes or less.

Base Stirfy Ingredients:
* Sesame oil
* Garlic
* Ginger
* Vegetables: onions, peppers, eggplant, carrots, radishes, zucchini, snow peas, kale, mustard greens, spinach, cabbage, mushrooms

Chop all of your vegetables and whisk up your stir-fry sauce. Heat up sesame oil in a skillet/pan/wok and add garlic and ginger for a minute, then throw in vegetables. Add sauce and sauté until softened.

Stir Fry Sauces

(Just whisk, whisk, whisk…)

Sweet and Sour

1/4 cup of water/chicken/or vegetable broth
2 Tbsp soy sauce
2 Tbsp cider, balsamic or rice wine vinegar
1 Tbsp brown sugar
1/2 tsp hot red pepper flakes

Chili-Lime

3 Tbsp sugar
3 Tbsp reduced sodium tamari (or soy sauce)
2 Tbsp fresh lime juice
2 Tbsp rooster red chili sauce
Garlic
Salt to taste

Ginger-Miso

3 Tbsp olive oil
Equal amounts of chopped garlic and ginger
2 Tbsp of yellow miso
1 Tbsp of soy sauce
1 Tbsp of rice vinegar
1/2 tsp sugar
Hot pepper flakes (to taste)

Roasted Vegetables

Homegrown vegetables don't need a whole lot of spices or stuff added to them—they taste that good. You'll be blown away by how amazing these simple roasted vegetables taste with just olive oil, salt and pepper. These make a great side dish.

Ingredients:
- Vegetables: any type of root vegetables—potatoes, turnips, beets, asparagus, cauliflower
- Olive oil
- Salt and pepper

Heat up oven to 375 degrees. Toss veggies in olive oil, and put on a cookie sheet. Add salt and pepper to taste. Roast for 15 minutes and then flip them over with a spatula. Roast for another 15 minutes or so until they are nicely browned.

Variation: Though you don't need any spices, a bit of curry powder on potatoes or cauliflower adds a nice touch.

ASPARAGUS
Grilled Asparagus

Ingredients:
- 1 pound fresh asparagus
- 1 Tbsp olive oil
- Salt and pepper to taste

Preheat grill. Lightly coat the asparagus spears with olive oil and season with salt and pepper to taste. Grill over high heat for 2 to 3 minutes, and serve right away.

BEANS
Crunchy Green Bean Pickles

These pickles stay totally crunchy, even after you can them. They also make a good match for a martini...

Ingredients:
- 2 1/2 pounds fresh green beans
- 2 1/2 cups distilled white vinegar
- 2 cups water
- 1/4 cup salt
- 1 clove garlic, peeled
- 1 bunch fresh dill weed
- 3/4 tsp red pepper flakes (optional)

Canning Recipe:
Sterilize 6 (1/2 pint) jars with rings and lids and keep hot. Trim green beans to 1/4 inch shorter than your jars. In a large saucepan, stir vinegar, water, and salt. Add garlic and bring to a rolling boil over high heat. In each jar, place 1 sprig of dill and 1/8 teaspoon of red pepper flakes. Pack green beans so they are standing on their ends.

Ladle the boiling brine into the jars, filling to within 1/4 inch of the tops. Discard garlic. Seal jars with lids and rings. Place in a hot water bath so they are covered by 1 inch of water. Simmer but do not boil for 10 minutes to process. Cool to room temperature. Test jars for a good seal by pressing on the center of the lid. It should not move. Refrigerate any jars that do not seal properly. Let pickles sit for two to three weeks before eating.

Variation: Wasabi Green Bean Pickles

Omg, these are good. Swap out the dill for 1 Tbsp of wasabi powder, and a few pieces of ginger for an added kick. These go great with a bloody mary.

BEETS
Main Course Beets

Have a heart, eat a beet instead as the main course. Thanks to Dave Keller for this one!

Ingredients:
* Beets
* Tinfoil
* Olive oil
* Salt and pepper to taste

Heat oven to 375 degrees. Skin beets, brush with a little bit of olive oil, and wrap completely in tinfoil. Bake for 40 minutes, until a knife goes through the beet. Serve with rice and greens.

Roasted Beet Salad

Ingredients:
* 10 medium sized red beets (washed)
* Dash of salt
* Sherry vinegar
* Some olive oil
* Fresh cracked pepper
* Some sour cream
* Fresh arugula (if you got it)

Place in covered roasting pan with 1/2 inch water and season with salt. Roast at 400 degrees for 1 hour or until knife glides through beets smoothly without resistance.

Remove from oven and let cool. With a pairing knife or towel you don't mind staining remove the skin from the beets. Once all beets are clean, cut the beets in quarters then slice. In a separate bowl add the beets, splash some Spanish sherry vinegar, olive oil, salt and fresh cracked pepper to taste.

Serve with sour cream (optional) and some fresh arugula.

CABBAGE

Raw cabbage is pretty awesome for you (Google it, you'll be amazed). Here are my two favorite recipes for getting your cabbage on.

Kraut

This is just like the super-expensive raw sauerkraut you see at the healthfood store. Oh, and it goes perfect with just about everything—sandwiches, picnics, or right out of the jar.

Ingredients:
*   Head of cabbage
*   1 1/2 tablespoons kosher salt

Plus:
*   Large 1/2 gallon Mason jar
*   Smaller pint Mason jar that fits inside large Mason jar
*   Lid for larger Mason jar

Wash cabbage, remove and save outer leaves, and slice thin or put in food processor to speed things up. Put in a bowl and add salt. Crunch it up with your hands to release the natural juices of the cabbage.

Keep crunching it for about 5 minutes or so. (Don't worry, this makes a lot and is so worth it).

Add the cabbage to the large sterilized Mason jar and push it down with a spoon. Keep pushing until liquid covers the cabbage completely. You don't want air to hit the kraut.

Add a large cabbage leaf to the top to seal it. Put smaller Mason jar inside large jar and push it down. Put a paper towel or piece of fabric over the whole thing and seal with your large Mason jar lid.

Let sit on your countertop for 3 to 4 days and make sure it stays submerged. (Air spoils the kraut). Taste on day 5 to see if it's done enough for you. It should be crunchy/salty and slightly tangy. If so, add to smaller sterilized Mason jars and put in the fridge.

Lasts up to 6 months and gets better the longer you wait.

Cabbage krauts faster when it's hot (above 72 degrees) so it will be done faster in the summer, and take longer in the winter.

Asian Slaw

Ingredients:

- Head of cabbage
- Carrots
- Bell peppers
- 1 Tbsp fresh ginger
- Radishes
- Cilantro
- 1/2 cup rice vinegar
- 2 tsp sesame oil
- 1 tsp of sugar (maple or agave work well too)
- Hot pepper (optional)

Chop chop everything (or food process it all) so it's matchstick size. In a separate bowl, whisk up rice vinegar, sugar, sesame oil, and hot pepper to taste. Pour over slaw and add chopped cilantro.

Keeps in the fridge for 5 days or so.

CARROTS
Carrot Pickles

Ingredients:

- 1/2 pound large carrots, peeled and cut longways.
- 1 tsp kosher or sea salt
- 1 cup unseasoned rice vinegar
- 3 Tbsp of sugar
- 1 cup water

Wash and cut carrots. Pat dry. In a pot, mix vinegar, salt, sugar, and water until the sugar dissolves, and heat up on the stove. While that's going, pack your carrots into sterilized Mason jars. Once the vinegar is boiling, pour it into the Mason jars to cover the carrots and seal. Let cool, then put in the fridge. These need to be refrigerated but they will stay crunchy, and are good for up to a month. Try making this with different colored carrots to really be a show off.

CAULIFLOWER
Cauliflowermash

Tastes just like potatoes! (Actually, it does.)

Ingredients:
* 1 head of cauliflower
* 1/4 cup of milk (can be hemp, nut or soymilk instead)
* 2 cloves of garlic
* Salt and pepper to taste

Cut up cauliflower and steam for 10 minutes. Once it's soft, put it in a food processor with milk and garlic and go for broke.

CUCUMBERS
Chilled Cucumber Salad

Ingredients:
* 3 medium size cucumbers
* 2 cloves of fresh garlic
* 1 shallot
* Fresh cilantro as a garnish
* 3 Tbsp of japanese rice wine vinegar (no RW vinegar on hand? Just mix 3 Tbsp of white vinegar with 6 tablespoons sugar and mix until sugar dissolves)
* 1 Tbsp soy sauce
* 1 tsp sesame oil

Slice cucumbers. Finely chop the garlic and shallot and mix it in with cucumbers. Add the rest of the ingredients. Toss several times to make sure all ingredients are mixed well. Let sit in refrigerator for a few hours before serving. Add slightly chopped cilantro as a garnish on top. If you like it spicy, add in some Sriracha hot sauce. One teaspoon to start and then add more if desired.

EGGPLANT
Baba Ganouj

I could live on this. The smoked version is amazing too. This gets smooth in a high speed blender so rock it if you got it. And, it freezes well, so make a lot!

Ingredients:
- 2 large eggplants
- 1/4 cup tahini
- 4 garlic cloves
- 1/4 cup fresh lemon juice
- Salt and pepper to taste
- Olive oil to brush eggplant
- Cumin

Heat oven to 375 degrees, cut eggplant in half, and prick the other side with a fork a few times. Brush eggplants with oil and cook until soft (about 20 minutes). With a spoon, scoop eggplant, sans skin, into a blender and add tahini, garlic, lemon juice, and spices. Blend. Cool. Enjoy. Now.

GARLIC
Roasted Garlic Spread

This fancy pants garlic spread is tasty and super healthy.

Ingredients:
- Head of garlic
- Olive oil
- Tinfoil

Heat up oven to 400 degrees. Take an entire head of garlic and cut the top off so you can just see the pointy heads. Drizzle with olive oil and wrap in foil. Bake for 20 minutes until soft.

Arrange on a plate with bread. Using a fork, pull out the softened cloves and spread on bread.

Quick Garlic Bread

Super quick way to give any piece of bread some garlicky goodness. It melts the garlic into the bread, like butter.

Ingredients:
* Peeled whole cloves of garlic
* Bread

Toast your bread. When bread is still warm, take garlic and scrape onto the bread, rotating so you use all sides.

KALE
Kale Chips

These are like get-out-of-jail-free potato chips, made of kale!
They have some serious crunch, are highly addictive, can be seasoned with whatever you want, and are usually expensive at the health food store. Here's how to make your own on the cheap.

Ingredients:
* Kale
* Olive oil
* Salt

Preheat oven to 350 degrees. Get a bunch of curly kale, wash, and then dry it with a salad spinner. Chop it up into chip size pieces, and mix in a bowl with olive oil and seasonings (don't over season, they do condense the flavor when they cook.). Arrange on a cookie sheet and cook for 10 to 15 minutes until the edges are browned, but not burnt.

Mix it up:
Add these different spices to make these kale chips your own:
* Cajun
* Nutritional yeast (to make them cheesy)
* Tamari

- Vinegar and salt
- Tahini, apple cider vinegar, lemon, and dash of soy sauce (tastes like bacon, kinda)

You can also put these in the dehydrator at 115 degrees for 4 hours to make raw kale chips.

Kale Tacos

Ingredients:
- Kale leaf
- Taco filling (beans, rice, guac, etc.)

Make a taco filling. Get a large kale leaf. Wrap it up and make a taco. Yum.

LETTUCE
3-simple salad dressings

Whisk these up in a bowl for a class act salad. They also will store in the fridge for up to a week if you have some left.

Lemon-Garlic Vinaigrette

1 cup extra virgin olive oil
4 cloves of garlic, pressed
2/3 cup lemon juice
2 teaspoons sugar
1/2 finely chopped green onion
1 teaspoon salt
1 teaspoon pepper

Balsamic Vinaigrette

3/4 cup olive oil
1/4 balsamic vinegar
2 cloves of pressed garlic
1/2 Dijon mustard
Spices: thyme, rosemary, and pepper work well
1 Tbsp sugar/honey/agave/or maple syrup

Miso Garlic Vinaigrette

1/4 cup white miso
3 Tbsp rice wine vinegar
2 cloves of garlic, pressed
1 Tbsp finely grated fresh ginger
1 1/2 tsps sugar/agave/honey or maple syrup
3 tsp plain (not toasted) sesame oil
1 Tbsp water

MELONS
Melon Yum Yum

Grab a spoon. Grab a melon. Cut melon in half. Eat. Yum.

Quick Blender Melon Sorbet

Who needs a fancy ice cream maker? I love that all you have to do is throw this in a blender for instant dessert! Stays good in the freezer for up to two weeks.

Ingredients:
* 1 melon
* Fine sugar
* Water

Remove seeds, scoop out melon, and cut into 1 inch squares or balls, and freeze. Once frozen get out blender, and add melon. Blend, adding sugar and a little bit of water if it needs help mixing up. Serve in a fancy glass, and call it a day.

Variations:

Add fresh mint leaves or lime juice to make it even more refreshing. Or, try basil leaves, or fresh strawberries. It's all *good*.

PEPPERS
Orange Crush Habanero Sauce

Using a blender is a great way to make short work of habaneros without chopping or burning your hands. But, still make sure to wear gloves—habaneros are no joke.

Ingredients:
- 20 whole habaneros (fresh or frozen) de-stemmed
- 1 cup apple cider vinegar
- 5 carrots, chopped
- 1 onion chopped
- 4 cloves of garlic
- 1 tsp olive oil
- Water to cover peppers
- Smoked paprika
- Salt and pepper
- Cumin
- 1 lime

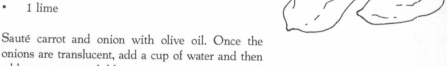

Sauté carrot and onion with olive oil. Once the onions are translucent, add a cup of water and then add your peppers. Add more water to just cover the peppers and let simmer for 5 minutes.

Once it's all softened, transfer (carefully!) to a blender (a Blendtec or Vitamix works great) and blend blend blend.

Then, move back to the stovetop and add apple cider vinegar and lime. Simmer until it thickens (about 10 more minutes.)

Put into hot sauce bottles and store in the fridge for up to a month, or freeze extra sauce in Mason jars. Then, get the water ready, this stuff is hot!

POTATOES
Beltzville Roasted Potatoes

Named after David Beltz of Beltzville, PA (a.k.a. trellis master of the Grow Indie Test Garden).

Ingredients:
- Potatoes
- A bunch of garlic
- Salt and Pepper
- Olive oil

Heat oven to 375 degrees, or get the grill going. Divide garlic into thirds and prepare the garlic 3 ways—mashed, rough chop, and course chop. Add extra virgin olive oil and cook for 1 minute. Then, add potatoes and mix it all up before adding salt and pepper. Check and turn potatoes every ten minutes until they are soft.

Variations
Home fries: Cut smaller
French Fries: Cut into French fry size, season with salt and olive oil.
Curry Fries: Add a few Tbsp of curry powder, turmeric, cumin and hot pepper.

SUMMER SQUASH
Zucchini Pasta

This super quick zucchini pasta is perfect for hot summer nights when you don't feel like cooking anything. You can throw a lot of labels on this dish (gluten-free, no fat, no carb, raw) but I just call it good. The zucchini takes on whatever spice/sauce you mix with it, and really does turn out like al dente pasta.

You'll need;
- Zucchini
- A potato peeler
- Salt and pepper to taste

Using a potato peeler, grate zucchini into fettuccini-like strips. Add your favorite sauce, pesto, mushrooms or just olive oil and fresh cherry tomatoes.

Variation: If you want to be all fancy, you can buy a zucchini spiralizer that makes perfect looking rotini pasta, or serrated vegetable peelers for a finer noodle. But a potato peeler works just fine at my house.

Steph's Zucchini Johnnie Cakes!

Every time my friend Stephanie brings these to a party, they are gone in like 5 minutes, no lie. They are that good.

Ingredients:
- 2 medium zucchini (about 1 pound)
- 2 Tbsp grated chopped onion
- 3 brown eggs, lightly beaten
- 5 Tbsp all-purpose flour
- 2 Tbsp corn meal
- Sea salt (to taste)
- 1/2 tsp freshly ground black pepper
- Sprinkle of paprika
- Butter and/or vegetable oil

Grate the zucchini into a bowl using the large grating side of a box grater. Immediately stir in the onion and eggs. Stir in 4 tablespoons of the flour, 1 tablespoon of the corn meal, salt, and pepper. If the batter gets too thin from the liquid in the zucchini, add the remaining 2 tablespoons of flour and corn meal. This is a wetter batter than regular pancakes.

Heat a large (10 to 12-inch) cast iron skillet over medium heat and melt 1/2 tablespoon butter and 1/2 tablespoon oil together in the pan. When the butter is hot but not smoking, lower the heat to medium-low and drop heaping spoonful of batter into the pan. Flatten each dollop so the middle gets done evenly with the edges. Sprinkle both sides with paprika. Cook the pancakes about 2-3 minutes on each side, until browned and the edges are crispy. Set aside to cool, and continue to add butter/oil to the pan and fry the pancakes until all the batter is used. Can be served warm or cool (I like them cool) and a dollop of sour cream slathered on top tastes divine!

Variation: Finely chopped bell peppers (in season the same time as zukes) are good to throw into the mix too.

TOMATOES
Easy, Amazing 20 Minute Tomato Sauce

I'm always amazed at the simplicity of this recipe, and that it can be on the table in a quick 20. Cooking or roasting your tomatoes this way really intensifies their flavor, making it a velvety rich sauce that's packed with good stuff.

It's also a great way to use all those cherry tomatoes. No need to skin and seed— an immersion blender will make short work of them.

Ingredients:

- A shoebox worth of homegrown tomatoes
- Olive oil
- Garlic
- Onion
- Salt
- Pepper
- Basil
- Lemon juice (if canning)
- Hot pepper (optional)

In a large pot on high heat, add a pinch of salt, let it warm up, then add the olive oil. Once fully heated, add onions and garlic until wilted. Then, add all of the tomatoes at once. Put on the lid and do something else for 20 minutes while it cooks down.

Once it's boiling and the tomatoes are soft, use an immersion blender to turn this into sauce. Cook down longer if you want a thicker sauce, or serve right away. This sauce is a great base. If you want to make it a puttnesca, add olives and capers. If you want to make it spicy, add a habanero. It's all up to you.

To can this sauce: Sterilize canning jars and squeeze half a lemon's juice into them. Add sauce, and boil water bath for 45 minutes. Try not to eat it until it's cold outside because it will be so good then!

Puttanesca Sauce

So what if puttanesca translates to hooker's sauce in Italian—this seductive sauce is all class. And quick to make (the ladies whipped this up in between "client meetings").

Ingredients:
- 10 large tomatoes, cored and chopped
- 1 onion, chopped
- 4 cloves garlic sliced thin (like in that *Goodfellas* prison scene)
- 1/3 cup pitted Kalamata olives
- 2 Tbsp capers
- 1/8 tsp red pepper flakes
- Two pinches fresh chopped herbs (parsley, basil, oregano, thyme)
- Dash of dry red wine
- Dash of balsamic vinegar

Sauté onion in olive oil until softened, add garlic for a minute, then throw in tomatoes, olives, and pepper flakes. Bring to a simmer. Add herbs, capers, and wine and balsamic to taste. Serve with pasta. Freezes well if you want to make extra.

Jeri's Tomato Pesto

This is a great way to store extra tomatoes, and so tasty on bread with fresh basil.

Ingredients:
- A bunch of tomatoes, sliced very thin
- 2 cloves of garlic (more or less what ever you like)
- 1/2 cup of walnuts (depends how nutty you like it)
- 1 1/2 cups of olive oil

Dehydrate your tomatoes—you can use a dehydrator or put them on a baking sheet in your oven at a very low setting. In a blender, mix up your garlic, olive oil, and walnuts till liquefied, then add the dehydrated tomatoes and blend until a thick paste. Store in the fridge or freeze in a Mason jar.

WINTER SQUASH
Pumpkin Gnocchi

This fancy sounding recipe works with any type of winter squash or even sweet potato, can be made quickly, and only takes 5 minutes to cook! Make a bunch and freeze half right before cooking by putting the gnocchis themselves on a tray in your freezer (so they don't stick together) then put in glass containers for later.

Ingredients:
- 2 cups of pumpkin puree
- 1 egg yolk (or egg substitute if vegan)
- 1 1/4 cup flour
- 1 tsp salt
- 2 Tbsp butter

Mix it all together, then, roll out, and cut into strips. Cut strips into squares and indent each with a fork. Boil water and cook for 5 minutes until they are floating on top. Drain, and use with what ever sauce you like.

Making the Most of Pumpkin/Squash Seeds

If you grew your own heirloom squash or pumpkin, save a few seeds for next year by washing them well, and drying them out on a plate. Then, sprinkle the rest of the seeds with olive oil, salt, and pepper and roast in the oven until crunchy (about 15 minutes, and flip them over a few times). Or, feed your extra seeds to any nearby chickens—they love em! Or, if it's that kinda day where extra seeds are stressing you out just put them in the compost pile. Seeds are pretty astounding things you know?

Spaghetti Squash Bowls

Just like pasta! Well, not exactly, but really it kind of is. Spaghetti squash is also gluten-free, low cal, and carb free—it's amazing that way.

Ingredients:
- Spaghetti squash
- Olive oil
- Salt and Pepper to taste

Heat oven to 400 degrees. Cut squash in half and remove seeds. Bake for 40 minutes or until soft. Take out and break up the squash with a fork to make spaghetti strands and use the shell as a bowl. Add whatever sauce you want. This dish works well with fresh chopped tomatoes, basil pesto, olives, artichokes, mushrooms, etc. Serve in the squash bowl and don't worry about doing the dishes tonight!

Chapter 8: Store

STORE

So, you spent all of this work growing stuff, scored some huge deal on a box of peppers at the farmer's market, and had a neighbor drop off tons of extra zucchini—now what?

It's easy to be overwhelmed at having a lot food in your house, especially if you have a small space or tiny apartment kitchen. Don't worry, there are plenty of options to make short work of that harvest and not waste a thing.

You'll be glad in December when you're cracking open those homemade pickles or making dinner for friends with homegrown heirloom tomato sauce that you can't get anywhere else.

MAKING PRODUCE LAST

Vegetables lose nutrients as time goes on, but, the good news is, unlike most veggies that have traveled thousands of miles, your own produce was just picked, and can last up to three weeks if you store it right.

Vegetable	Best way to store fresh
Asparagus	Put in a cup of water, or wrap in a wet paper towel and place in a bag in the fridge
Beans	Place unwashed beans in plastic bags in the crisper
Beets	Cut off tops and store in sealed plastic bag in the fridge
Broccoli	Store unwashed in a plastic bag in the fridge
Cabbage	Store unwashed in a plastic bag in the fridge
Carrots	Remove tops and store in jars of water in the fridge. Will last for over a week this way if you replace the water every 3 days

Vegetable	Best way to store fresh
Cauliflower	Store unwashed in a plastic bag in the fridge
Celery	Wash, cut, and put in an airtight container in the fridge
Corn	Corn is best eaten soon as it's picked. Freeze it if you can't eat it within a day or two
Cucumber	Store unwashed in a plastic bag in the fridge
Eggplant	Paper bag in the fridge
Kale	Store unwashed in a plastic bag in the fridge
Lettuce	Store unwashed in a plastic bag in the fridge
Melons	Keep at room temp and eat as fresh as possible
Onions	Store in a mesh bag at room temp.
Peas	Eat quickly after picking, or store in loose plastic bags in the fridge
Peppers	Clean and store in containers in the fridge. Can even be washed and chopped before being stored, so they are ready for anything
Potatoes	Store in a ventilated paper bag away from light
Radishes	Cut greens and roots off, wash, and store in a bowl of fresh water in the fridge
Spinach	Wash and air dry, then store in an airtight container in the fridge
Summer Squash	Wash and store in a plastic bag in the fridge
Tomatoes	Wash and store at room temperature
Winter Squash and Pumpkins	Wipe clean and store at room temperature

Source: Iowa State University Horticulture Guide

INFUSIONS

Homemade infusions are a great way to use up herbs and make fancy schmancy oils and vinegars. Or, spice up that traditional bloody mary with your own habanero infused vodkas at your next brunch. These also make fantastic presents and are a great way to enjoy the garden all year long. Get on it.

How it works: The vinegar, oil or alcohol draws out the flavor of the herb and infuses it into the liquid, which acts as a preservative. To preserve these for the long haul, sterilize your glass bottles first steaming them in a pot of boiling water for 10 minutes.

Flavored Vinegars

These herbal vinegars are good for salads, marinating, adding to soups, or just adding a little oomph to whatever's on the stove.

For every 2 cups of vinegar, use three to four sprigs of fresh herbs, or 3 tablespoons of dried herbs. Heat up vinegar in a non-aluminum pot and remove just before it starts to boil. Put your fresh herbs in a large glass jar and cover with your hot vinegar. Put a lid on it and let sit in a dark spot for two weeks before straining into smaller bottles. Add a few fresh herbs (just for nice) and label. Store in the fridge after opening.

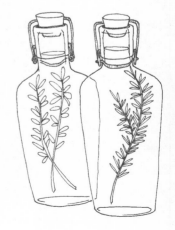

Flavored Oils

These are also great for making your own cooking oils, and the flavor combos are endless. (Although, don't use garlic for oils, it doesn't keep well.) Just take half a cup of fresh herbs for every 3 cups of oil (olive, sesame, or any light oil will do), put the lid on and place in a sunny window for ten days to help it infuse. Label and use within two months.

Flavored Alcohol

Start by buying some cheap alcohol (the flavor of your infusion will take over, so buying fancy vodka kind of defeats the purpose, but if you want to spend some bucks, go for it. I go mid- to bottom-shelf) Add your herbs, peppers, or whatever you plan on using and place in a dark area to infuse. Shake a few times each day and infuse for two weeks, or to taste. Strain into final glass bottles, and label.

Mix it Up

You can infuse any type of fresh herb with vinegar, oil or alcohol, so have fun experimenting.

Some good infusions include:
* Garlic, Rosemary, and Marjoram
* Savory, Thyme, Oregano,
* Garlic Basil
* Chili peppers

Reused wine or liquor bottles are perfect for infusions, and you can make your own labels and give them out as gifts.

CANNING

Ah, canning, that age-old tradition. Canning is a good way to store (or "put up") a large amount of food for a long time, without having to refrigerate or freeze it. When you can something, you kill all of the food-spoiling organisms, and create an airtight seal to preserve the food for up to 5 years.

There are two types of canners—pressure canners and water bath canners.

Water bath canning is traditionally used for canning fruits (including tomatoes) and is easier to do than pressure canning (which is typically done for vegetables). There is a lot of debate in the canning world in regards to which way is safer/easier to use, but I water bath tomatoes, pickles, chutneys, jellies, and salsas, and freeze straight up vegetables to keep things simple.

What You Need:

-A canning kit (this includes a large lobster-type pot, a rack for holding your jars, and a jar lifter.)

Or
-A large pot, jars, lids, and twisty ties

If you don't have a traditional canning set, it's easy to make one. Just get a large soup pot (big enough to hold at least four jars and submerge them). Then, get a few extra Mason jar bands and tie them together and put them on the bottom of your pot. The idea is you do not want the jars to touch the bottom of they pot; they sit on the lids instead, and should be 1/2 inch or more off the bottom.

First, fill your pot a little more than halfway. While that's going, get another pot and fill it a quarter of the way with water, put your canning jars, lids, and bands in the second and pot steam to sterilize.

Once steamed, take out and add whatever you want canned.

Put canning jars, with lids and bands, in the large pot of boiling water and process for as long as your recipe calls for. Make sure water covers the jar lids by at least an inch.

Once done, take out and let cool. You'll hear the signature "pop" for a while as the jars seal. Place on the shelf. Anything that didn't seal, eat right away.

time to spoon!

screw 'em!

check it

YOU CAN CAN

The Dreaded Botch

Botulism is one of those things that you hear about a lot, but no one knows anyone that has got it. For all the hubbub, you'd think it was common, but it's rare—according to the CDC, only about 20 people get it each year in the U.S., and that's because they tried to can low acid vegetables (like asparagus).

Not that that means you should take risks. Botulism spores can survive when you don't process your canned food enough, or you don't have high enough acid content in your food.

Luckily, fruits (including tomatoes) are high in acid, but to be safe, you can add a few tablespoons of lemon juice to each jar. For pickles, no need to worry, because the vinegar raises the acid level.

Adjusting Canning Times for Altitude
1,000 to 3,000 feet above sea level—add 5 minutes
3,000 to 6,000 feet above sea level—add 10 minutes
6,000 to 8,000 feet above sea level—add 15 minutes

PICKLING

In the days before refrigeration, supermarkets, and mass industrialized canning machines, if you wanted to store your harvest, pickling was the way to go. This age old practice dates back to 2030 BC, but don't let that intimidate you—it's fun to make your own pickles.

And I'm not sure if you knew, but there are two types of pickles:

Vinegar Pickling: The first type preserves vegetables in vinegar solution that is then water bath sterilized to keep out bad bacteria (think crunchy sandwich pickles).

Fermentation: The second type of pickling, known as lacto-fermentation, uses salt or whey to encourage the growth of good bacteria (like sauerkraut and kimchi). These are not heated up or pasteurized in any way, they simply let the good bacteria do its stuff.

DIY Pickles
We're not talking about those pasteurized pickles you find lining the deli section at the supermarket that have traveled from who knows where and are filled with Yellow #5 and Blue #1—homemade pickles are much tastier and healthier for you, there won't be any turning back.

Think outside the cucumber!
There are a million different types of pickle variations, and you can pickle anything you grow.

How to Pickle Anything
Works with any vegetable, but great with crunchy ones, like cucumbers, beets, brussel sprouts, green beans, etc.

4 lbs any vegetables
2 3/4 cups apple cider vinegar
3 cups water
1/4 cup non-iodized sea salt
3 tablespoons coriander seeds

12 dried chilies (optional)
3 tablespoons cumin seeds
3 tablespoons mustard seeds
12-24 garlic cloves
(Optional: other spices to taste!)
Makes 6 pints

Sterilize jars by boiling them for 10 minutes. Set aside.

Combine vinegar, water and salt and bring to a boil. Put vegetables, and 1 chili pepper, 1 to 2 cloves of garlic, a pinch of cumin, coriander, and mustard seeds into sterilized canning jars.

Pour the vinegar mixture over the vegetables to 1/4" from the top of the jar. Process in hot water bath canner for 10 minutes. Store out of direct sunlight and wait six weeks before opening.

Easy One Step Refrigerator Pickles

Don't have time to drag the canner out? Make pickles in just 10 minutes with this simple refrigerator recipe. They will stay crunchy, and keep in the fridge for up to two months.

6 cups chopped or sliced vegetables (cucumbers, beets, carrots, radishes, etc.)
1 onion, thinly sliced
2 cups white vinegar
1/4 cup sugar
3/4 teaspoon salt
1/2 teaspoon mustard seeds
4 garlic cloves, sliced
Makes 4 pints

Optional spices to add to jars: Dill, habanero/pepper flakes, peppercorns, whatever you like!

Pack vegetables, spices, and garlic cloves in sterilized glasses. Combine vinegar and sugar in a small saucepan, stir well and bring to a boil. Cook 1 minute and pour into jars. Put lids on, let it cool for an hour and keep jars in the fridge. Let cure for 4 days then it's fair game. Yum!

FERMENTING

In today's time pressed and pasteurized obsessed-world, fermenting may be intimidating to some folks, but it's a safe and easy process that's very good for you. It can be as simple as putting chopped vegetables in a Mason jar for a few days, then storing them in a cold area—like the fridge—after they've fermented. And don't freak out about eating foods that are sitting out for a few days—it's a natural process that's good for you. If you've eaten yogurt, had sourdough bread, or drank a beer, you've had fermented foods.

The lactic acid created through the fermentation process (a.k.a. lacto-fermenting) is a natural preservative that creates healthy bacteria that improves digestion. Generations ago, everyone ate fermented foods, and this probiotic bacteria is greatly missing from today's standard American diet.

Fermented foods are filled with probiotics, enzymes, vitamins, minerals and digestive enzymes that work to break down your food, supporting the absorption of vitamins and minerals. If you have a bad Buddha belly, fermented foods can help. Some people say it can help treat depression, autism, Crohn's, etc.

Any vegetable can be fermented, and it's a great way to store and use up extra greens, cabbage, carrots, garlic, radishes, beets, you name it. Here are a few lacto-fermented foods you can make:

Fermented cabbage dishes:
Sauerkraut and kimchi
Condiments: Chutneys, marmalade, fruit butter, preserves, and mustards
Pickled Vegetables: Beets, carrots, garlic, onion, greens, etc.

← fancy

How to Ferment Any Vegetable

Fermented vegetables have started becoming an artisan craft, and they can be quite expensive. Here's an easy way to make your own for a fraction of the price:

- Chop, cut, grate or food process any raw vegetable.
- Put veggies in a large mixing bowl, add a tablespoon of salt and start kneading and breaking it up with your hands.
- Add another tablespoon if you have a large batch and keep breaking it until the vegetables are really sweating.
- Transfer the vegetables into glass Mason jars.
- Pack it down so the liquid covers the veggies.

- Put on jar lids and bands and let it sit for 3 to 5 days. Move it to the fridge when it's to your liking.

How much salt to add? Try 3 tablespoons of salt per 5 pound of vegetables.

Fermenting foods like it on the warmer side (70 degrees+), so it may take longer to cure if it's cold in your house. In the winter months, you can wrap the container in a towel and place it inside an insulated or thermal chest to give your fermented veggies some extra love. In the summer months, you'll notice they culture faster and may be ready in 2 to 3 days.

Lacto-fermented vegetables improve with maturation and will last several months in the fridge. If you open a jar and see bubbly foam on top, don't freak out, that's normal. Scoop it off.

FREEZING

Freezing food is a lifesaver for the busy gardener, especially in the summer when it's a million degrees out and the last thing you want to do is stand in front of a hot pot of boiling water.

If you don't have a lot of pantry space for canned or dried stuff, a chest freezer is a great option because they hold a lot of food. Most things will keep for six months without losing flavor. You can also freeze cooked tomato sauces, ketchups, hot sauces, chutneys, and pesto very easily instead of canning.

How it works: Freezing stops the enzymes and microorganisms that break down food in their tracks—like cryogenics! When frozen properly, vegetables keep most of their nutrients and vitamins intact, so you have the next healthiest thing to fresh.

Freezing in Mason Jars

You don't have to freeze your food in those chintzy, BPA-filled plastic containers—glass canning jars work great for freezing and storing food. Score some quart-size glass Mason jars at the supermarket, or even at yard sales for cheap. They can be reused over and over again and don't make your food taste like plastic.

When filling your glass jars, don't overfill— leave an inch of headspace because food expands when frozen and you don't want them to break. I've been freezing and refreezing the same jars for years and I haven't broken a jar yet!

I use Mason jars for everything—storing leftovers, bringing an ice coffee to the garden, or as a water bottle. Plastic is filled with tons of nasty chemicals that leach into whatever it holds, and then all those bottles end up in some landfill or ocean. Glass can be reused over and over, it doesn't leach at all, it's 100% recyclable. And it's classy.

How to Freeze

With the exception of whole tomatoes, peppers, and herbs like basil, dill, and parsley, all vegetables should be blanched first to lock in more vitamins, preserve their color, and prevent them from getting a funky texture. No one wants mushy vegetables! Here's how:

First, Prep: It's easiest to gather and prep your crop by vegetable, and process and store each type individually. Start by washing, and cutting your vegetables.

To Blanch: Boil a large pot of water. In a separate bowl, prepare an ice bath by filling the bowl with water and adding ice. When the pot of water is boiling, add your vegetable and boil for the appropriate time. Using a colander or slotted spoon, remove the vegetables from the boiling water and place in the ice bath. Then, remove vegetables from the cold water and add to freezer bags.

Mark your bags or containers well—food can go incognito after it's frozen and you might not recognize it!

To Defrost

Just take your frozen item out the night or morning before and let it defrost in the fridge. You can also do a quick defrost by putting the jars or bag in another bowl of warm water and it will thaw in about an hour.

Blanching times

Vegetable	How many Minutes to Blanch
Asparagus	2 (small), 3 (medium), 4 (large)
Beans-Pole	3
Beans-Bush	2 (small), 3 (medium), 4 (large)
Beets	Cook first
Broccoli	3
Brussel Sprouts	5 for Large heads, 3 for small
Cabbage or Chinese Cabbage	1 and 1/2
Carrots	5 for small, 2 for Diced or strips
Cauliflower	3
Celery	3
Corn	7 (small ears), 9 (medium), 11 (large)
Eggplant	4
greens	3 for collards, 2 for all others
onions	
(blanch until center is heated)	3-7
Rings	10-15 seconds
Peas-Edible Pod	1 and 1/2 to 3
Peas-field (blackeye)	2
Peas-Green	1 and 1/2
Peppers	freeze without blanching
Potatoes	3 to 5
Soybeans-Green	5
Squash-Summer	3
Sweet Potatoes	Cook thoroughly, Don't blanch
Tomatoes	freeze without blanching
Winter squash and Pumpkins	Cook thoroughly, Don't blanch

Source: Cooperative Extension Service, The University of Georgia, Athens.

Freezing herbs:

Enjoy your own homegrown herbs all winter long! They are easy to freeze (no blanching required). Wash, chop them up, and put them in ice cube trays. Then, fill each cube with water and throw the tray in the freezer. Once it's frozen, divide it out in individual bags and label them.

The next time you are making a sauce, soup or curry, you can just pull out a bag of herbs and drop an ice cube in.

DRYING

Drying is one of the oldest methods of preserving food, and also one of the simplest ways to stock up. In addition to drying vegetables and fruits, you can also easily dry your own herbs and teas to enjoy the garden year-round.

How it works: By removing all of the moisture in a vegetable, you inhibit the growth of the microorganisms that age food, allowing you to store dried food well into the gardening season. Drying preserves the enzymes in vegetables, making them a living food.

If done right, dried food has more nutrients than canning, retaining its flavor and color for up to a year or more. Dried foods also look great stored in Mason jars in the pantry.

There are several ways to dry your harvest:

Dehydrators: A dehydrator is a small oven with a fan that cooks at low temperatures and dries food without killing the beneficial enzymes. Dehydrators can be expensive, but are a good investment because they are a fool proof way to dry out and store your food. Plus raw foodies (who don't eat food cooked above 118 degrees) can use a dehydrator for making all sorts of stuff, from living flax seed crackers to fruit leathers and yummy kale chips. (See recipe on page 95.)

Regular Oven on Low:
Don't have a food dehydrator? No problem, you can use a regular oven, placed on its lowest setting (but no higher than 180 degrees) with the door propped open so moisture can escape. Spread out the veggies/herbs on a cookie sheet and bake for 3 to 4 hours, checking every hour to make sure they aren't scorched. Once dried, let cool and store in Mason jars or freezer containers.

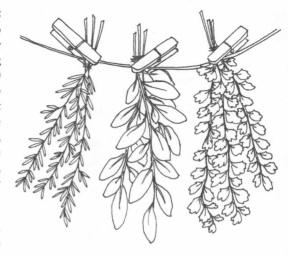

Solar Drying: If you live in a hot, dry climate where it gets over 85 degrees, you can use the power of the sun to dry fruits (including tomatoes, yum). Arrange your fruit in a single layer between two fine mesh screens and stack this under a glass window frame. Place directly in the sun for two or three days and bring inside at night. Don't worry about birds or bugs, the top rack will prevent them from hijacking your drying fruit. Or, go totally analog and use your car—just wait for a hot day, crack the windows, and lay your food racks on the dash.

Air Drying Herbs: Drying herbs is simple, so if you have the opportunity to pick a ton of basil or oregano from your CSA or garden, go for it—they dry and store well! Pick your herbs and arrange a bunch of them, tying the cut end with a rubber band. Then, gently wash the herbs and tie up in a dry place, upside down.

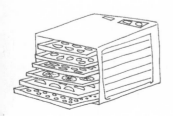

Keep it Fresh
Don't use overripe fruit or veggies that are on their way out—they won't be any better dried out. Harvest right before you dry for best taste and nutrients.

RESOURCES
Books

- *Square Foot Gardening*, Mel Bartholomew, 1981
- *Lasagna Gardening*, Patricia Lanza, 1998
- *How to Grow More Vegetables: Than You Ever Thought Possible on Less Land Than You Can Imagine*, John Jeavons, 1995
- *Jeff Ball's 60-Minute Vegetable Garden: Just One Hour a Week for the Most Productive Vegetable Garden Possible*, Jeff Ball, 1992
- *Four-Season Harvest: Organic Vegetables from Your Home Garden All Year Long*, Elliot Coleman, 1999
- *The Self-Sufficient Suburban Gardener*, Jeff Ball, 1983

Seeds
Baker Creek Heirloom Seed Company
The place for heirlooms, Baker Creek Seed Company features more than 1,400 different beautiful heirloom varieties.
www.rareseeds.com

Blackbird Naturals
Offering organic, heirloom garden, and superfood seeds from California.
www.blackbirdnaturals.com

Fedco Seeds
Great Northeast Maine company that sells seed in large and trial-size packets so you can try out a bunch of seeds on the cheap. They also sell great potatoes through Moose Tubers.
www.fedcoseeds.com

Happy Cat Farm
A great selection of heirloom beans, tomatoes, and homesteading supplies.
www.happycatorganics.com

High Mowing Seeds
This cool indie seed company in Vermont features over 500 varieties of certified organic vegetable, open pollinated herb and flower seeds.
www.highmowingseeds.com

Localharvest.org
Buy seeds directly from indie growers across the country.
www.localharvest.org

Sustainable Seed Company
This California-based heirloom seed company, offers a great selection of heirloom vegetable seeds, along with unique varieties of grain, tobacco, cover crops, and more.
www.sustainableseedco.com

Renee's Garden
Heirloom and hybrid flower, herb and vegetables seeds that are super easy to grow. Renee's sells great variety mixes and garden collections so you can try a lot of new varieties without having to spend a lot on individual seed packets.
www.reneesgarden.com

Seeds of Italy
A generous selection of authentic Italian seeds, with hard-to-find culinary varieties of basil, tomatoes, squash, arugula, and tons more.
www.growitalian.com

Seeds of Change
Offering more than 1,200 certified organic seed varieties for the home gardener and market-grower.
www.seedsofchange.com

Seed Saver's Exchange
Features rare varieties and heirlooms. A non-profit seed organization dedicated to saving and sharing seeds around the country.
www.seedsavers.org

Territorial Seed Company
Family owned seed company with a good selection of heirlooms, grains, potatoes, garlic and plants.
www.territorialseed.com

Underwood Gardens
Good selection of heirloom vegetable, herb and flower seeds.
www.underwoodgardens.com

Homesteading Supplies

Tribest
Featuring primo juicers, dehydrators, wheatgrass kits, yogurt and nut milk makers, grain mills, and anything else you need to make healthy food from your garden.
www.tribest.com

Home Food Processing
All-things homesteading, here you can find fermenting pots, all metal dehydrators, beer/wine making equipment, cabbage shredders, and more.
www.home-food-processing.com

Lehman's
Located in Ohio's Amish Country, this store has a great selection of homesteading stuff.
www.lehmans.com

Canning Jars and lids
Tattler BPA-free Reusable Canning Lids
Most Mason jar lids have BPA, but Tattler lids are BPA-free, and they work with your existing Mason jars. Plus, you can reuse them.
www.reusablecanninglids.com

Weck Canning Jars
These BPA-free jars are so pretty, and you never have to buy lids!
www.weckcanning.com

Growing

Earthbox
Self-watering patio container garden that can grow lots of food in a small box.
www.earthbox.com

Gardener's Supply
Great selection of raised beds, grow bags, seed starting kits and gardening tools.
www.gardeners.com

Garden's Alive

A comprehensive selection of organic fertilizers, pesticides, garden tools, raised beds, and more.
www.gardensalive.com

Garden Tool Co.

Every possible gardening tool you can imagine.
www.gardentoolcompany.com

Herb Kits

Good selection of medicinal, cooking and herbal tea indoor herb garden kits.
www.herbkits.com

Indoor Grow Lights

Great selection of adjustable indoor plant lights.
www.buyplantlights.com

Potted

Stylish collection of modern garden furniture, supplies, books, and more.
www.pottedstore.com

Scout Regalia

DIY raised bed kits and free downloadable plans to make your own.
www.scoutregalia.com

Sprout Home

Modern garden planters accessories, and sustainable furniture with urban garden style.
sprouthome.stores.yahoo.net

Sustainable Seed Company

Good selection of organic fertilizers, organic gardening products and heirloom seeds.
www.sustainableseedco.com

Terrain

Boutique gardening shop featuring a lovely selection of garden gear, containers, books, planters and more.
www.shopterrain.com

The Big Tomato

Big selection of growing supplies, nutrients, and products for the indoor gardener.
www.thebigtomato.com

Urban Worms

Offering vermicomposting kits for any space, free resources and articles about turning your table scraps into garden-loving, worm food.
www.urban-worms.com

Wolly Pocket

Vertical gardening and modular wall growing systems perfect for city/apartment dwellers.
www.woollypocket.com

ABOUT US

Part foodie, part agrarian, and all rabble rouser, Robyn Jasko started her blog Grow Indie in 2009 to give people the tools, know-how and moxie to grow their own food. Although she's lived everywhere, from a llama farm in the country to a tiny brownstone in the city, she's always managed to have a garden, even if it was just a small fire escape tomato plant. In 2010, she and her friend, Colleen Underwood started a community garden in their town so everyone could have a space to grow stuff. In 2012, after planting way too many habanero plants and heirloom garlic, Homesweet Homegrown Hot Sauces was born.

Robyn has tried to grow almost everything. (Although we are still waiting to sprout an avocado successfully). She lives with her partner in crime, Paul David, and their son Ajax at their homesweet home in Kutztown, PA. Find her at homesweethomegrown. com and growindie.com.

Born in 1986, Jenn spent her childhood gluing things to cats, collecting bits of string and eating rock salt. Eventually she got tired of trying to avoid people on Facebook and built a rocket ship out of tin cans, which only made it as far as the greater Kempton, PA area. There she established the Astrobase with space engineer and dirty potter, R.Poppy. She gets schooled in the ways of weaving and fiber arts at Kutztown University.

Currently Jenn occupies her time by drawing silly cartoons, making gluten-free food stuffs, and wearing googly eyes.

SUBSCRIBE TO EVERYTHING WE PUBLISH!

Do you love what Microcosm publishes?

Do you want us to publish more great stuff?

Would you like to receive each new title as it's published?

Subscribe as a BFF to our new titles and we'll mail them all to you as they are released!

$10-30/mo, pay what you can afford. Include your t-shirt size and month/date of birthday for a possible surprise! Subscription begins the month after it is purchased.

microcosmpublishing.com/bff

...AND HELP US GROW YOUR SMALL WORLD!